Not ✳ ✳ ✳
As
Orphans

Not As Orphans

Scenes, Reflections, Meditations & Prayers
On Intimacy With God

Allyn Benedict

iUniverse, Inc.
Bloomington

NOT AS ORPHANS
Scenes, Reflections, Meditations & Prayers On Intimacy With God

Scripture taken from the HOLY BIBLE, NEW INTERNATIONAL VERSION ®. NIV®. COPYRIGHT © 1973, 1978, 1984 by International Bible Society. Used by permission. All rights reserved worldwide. Additional scripture taken from The Message by Eugene H. Peterson, copyright © 1993, 1994, 1995, 1996, 2000, 2001, 2002. Used by permission of NavPress Publishing Group. All rights reserved.

iUniverse books may be ordered through booksellers or by contacting:

iUniverse
1663 Liberty Drive
Bloomington, IN 47403
www.iuniverse.com
1-800-Authors (1-800-288-4677)

ISBN: 978-1-4697-8192-1 (sc)
ISBN: 978-1-4697-8193-8 (ebk)

Printed in the United States of America

iUniverse rev. date: 02/24/2012

I will not leave you as orphans; I will come to you. Before long, the world will not see me anymore, but you will see me. Because I live, you also will live. On that day you will realize that I am in my Father, and you are in me, and I am in you.

John 14:18-20

✳ ✳ ✳

To the coming of the Kingdom of God the Father, who gave me this new heart and who renews it daily with his faithful, truthful, merciful loving. And to my wife, Jude, who knows and has my heart as no other human companion ever could.

✳ ✳ ✳

$\mathcal{C}$ontents

CHAPTER THREE

CHAPTER FOUR

𝒜uthor's Note

The subject of this book is a life of intimacy with God. It is my hope that it will have clear "practical" value. The degree to which it is practical for *you* will depend upon what it is you seek and where you intend to go in your spiritual life. This book will have practical application if you desire to move into new and more vital dimensions of a personal relationship with God. I believe it will be of help to you if you desire to yield more and more to the will of God, and to his embrace of love and mercy. But my greatest hope is that *Not as Orphans* will be a place of meeting between you and the living God: Father, Son and Holy Spirit.

Each of the four chapters of *Not as Orphans* focuses on a different aspect or characteristic of that restored relationship with God which, in the Gospel of John, Jesus calls "eternal life". All four chapters have the same structure: dramatic scenes with reflections—each followed by devotional material—alternate with Psalm meditations. Each chapter concludes with a prayer response to scripture.

Concerning the 'dramatic scenes' with reflections and devotional material: The scenes are, in a sense, "windows" through which we see illustrated some facet(s) of a life of intimacy with God. The chapters begin with an original scene. The other two scenes in each chapter are simply presented as they occur in scripture, with the exception of the scene from the book of Isaiah (in Chapter 2) which I have dramatized. These dramatic foundations, then, serve as "jumping off places" for the reflections which follow. The reflections are not point-by-point commentaries, nor is their scope entirely limited to that of the scenes they follow. At the end of each reflection I have provided brief summary notes and some questions for private or group reflection and/or discussion, which may serve as paths into deeper understanding and more personal application.

Concerning the psalm meditations: You are encouraged to read the psalm first. However, each meditation is headed by a quotation from the psalm, which draws the reader's attention to the *primary* focus of the meditation. While the content of each meditation amplifies, to some extent, an aspect of the theme of the chapter in which it appears, the connection is not necessarily simple or obvious. All, however, are rooted in the *overall* theme of the book: a life of intimacy with God.

Concerning the prayers: The scriptural subject of these prayers is a passage from the Gospel of John [14:18-20]. I pray into the first sentence of the scripture in the first chapter, the second sentence in the second chapter, and so on. This scripture is the root passage for the entire book from the title to the last words of the Epilogue.

Finally, an invitation: if you find yourself tempted to laugh occasionally, I would invite you to yield. Laughter is a great place to meet with the Lord who, I hope you have discovered, gives his children the gift of a wonderfully cleansing and liberating grace in the *sacrament* of humor!

𝒫rologue

Psalm 42 begins: "As a deer pants for streams of water, so my soul pants for you, O God. My soul thirsts for God, for the living God." Peterson paraphrases it this way in *The Message*: "A white-tailed deer drinks from the creek; I want to drink God, deep draughts of God. I'm thirsty for God-alive."

There is no doubt that God desires hunger and thirst in his people: spiritual hunger—spiritual thirst. We need living bread, but we would not seek the bread if we did not experience the hunger. We would starve spiritually, just as we would starve physically if all experience of hunger was gone and we were not driven to eat by the experience of emptiness.

We need living water, but unless we experience thirst for God, our spiritual life becomes a dry place where nothing can grow. Our Heavenly Father sees that desert in us and desires that we know thirst, not because he desires discomfort for us, but because he knows what we need and wants to reign in our hearts.

There is a stream in him where we can soak—where hearts and minds and spirits can come alive and sprout a great harvest. There is a way into the never-failing stream of his life. It is the way of thirst. There is a path leading to bread for the life that will not pass away. It is the path of hunger.

These are gifts of God. We cannot make ourselves hungry or thirsty for God, but we can "thirst after thirst": we can desire those gifts, ask for them, and receive them. When we do, we discover that the water is indeed living water. The bread is living bread. We drink of him. We are nourished by his Body. He is the giver and he is the gift.

Do you know you are hungry? Do you know you are thirsty? If you do, give thanks! Then come to the table that God is providing and be satisfied.

"At The Foot Of The Cross": A Vision

I find myself on a beautiful hillside in Galilee. There is a large crowd gathered. Jesus is here. He has come to teach. As I sit waiting expectantly among the people, I find myself thinking about how I have grown in wisdom and understanding over the course of these past three years. Wherever Jesus has taught, I have been there to learn. I am eager to hear Jesus, but I am not at all anxious. I am comfortable. I know that most of his words and his deep penetrating looks will be directed to those around me, who have not heard him before.

Because I have heard him teach so many times, I think I know what he will say. His words will be words of conviction, truth, hope and healing. I have seen Jesus touch lives in many ways. He will give them something unexpected and wonderful. The radiant love that shines from him will enter their hearts as pure gift.

Yet he sees beneath the surface and I know he will lovingly challenge them to become aware of all the subtle ways of sin that form the pattern of their lives. I have seen many hearts changed through repentance.

Jesus opens his mouth to speak, but I am suddenly disoriented. The world has become strange. The sound of his voice takes a long time to reach me, and when his words finally arrive, they are not the words I expected. Surely these hard words cannot be his. My heart and my mind are racing. I look to see if this is actually Jesus speaking.

His voice comes with great power, searing my mind and heart. I am flooded with shame and fear and guilt. I know beyond knowing that if I accept these words as truth then the very ground that has supported my life will be shaken and I will enter into a place of pain and chaos.

Then, as though I have suddenly woken, I realize that we are not on a green hill and Jesus has not even begun to speak. All he has done is look at me. With a shock I see that this look is coming from the eyes of a man in agony, nailed to a cross. In his eyes I see that he knows me. I cannot move.

I cannot put any distance between this crucifixion and me. It is taking place here and now. I am at the foot of the cross. I look down. There is blood on my hands and the unendurable, crushing weight of shame and guilt on my heart.

My eyes are drawn to his eyes again. Then Jesus speaks to me for the first time: "I forgive you". There is no way to explain the healing, freeing power of these words. "I love you", he says, "Come close to me."

I am a long time there with him on that barren, rocky hill. The stones cry out in praise. There are no more words. There is just this time.

*C*hapter One

INTIMACY:
A place where we meet in truth
to give and to receive

An intimate relationship with God is experienced and lived out as we meet with him where we are and as we are. In that place of meeting, God desires to receive us and to give himself to us. And God invites us to receive and give ourselves to him.

SCENE: "WHERE WERE YOU?"

Let us imagine that you and I have agreed to meet next Wednesday in the sanctuary of our church at 12:00 noon. You arrive 5 minutes early and begin to wait. I never show up. You wait for 30 minutes, then leave.

You call me that night and ask, "Where were you?"

"Oh," I say, "I was out of town."

"Out of town! Was it an emergency?"

"No."

"A last-minute thing?"

"No."

"You mean you've known all along you couldn't be there?"

"Uh huh."

"Do you mean to tell me that you knew you couldn't show up because you were going to be somewhere else but you actually made an appointment with me anyway?"

"Yup!"

"Why would you do that?"

"Well," I say, "I really wanted to be in the church and I looked forward to some quiet time with you. But it was more than that: I had met with Fred there last week and it was special . . . . I felt as though I was supposed to be there again."

"Hold on. Let me get this straight. You wanted to be there, but it wasn't possible?"

"Right."

"You thought God wanted you to be there but you had this other place you knew you were going to go instead?"

"Right."

"But you weren't about to let that small problem get in the way? You went ahead and made an appointment with me!"

"Exactly."

"But . . . but . . . but . . . ," you sputter, "but how . . . but what . . . but . . . it couldn't possibly work out! You knew it couldn't! Why would you do something like that"?

"Well, it's where I wanted to be. I really thought I ought to be there. And I'd been there before and . . ."

"Alright—OK—fine! We've already been through that garbage!"

You pause. You calm yourself. You are searching for just the right words. Finally you have them:

"You know what?"

"What?"

"You're a fool!"

"Thank you very much."

"No, really, I mean it."

"I said thanks."

"I don't want your thanks. What I want is that the next time we make an appointment, we make it for some place where you're going to be at the time!"

"Interesting. Sounds good."

"You think you'll do it then?"

"Well, I'd like to. I ought to."

"But will you?"

"Probably not."

"I thought so."

"So," I say, "when would you like to get together?"

Finally you have me. You ask, "How about right now!"

"Well, I really should—and don't get me wrong, I'd love to—but I need to go . . . have to spend some time with the wife. She's been waiting for me!"

"You're going to meet with her now?"

"No. Afraid not. I have another appointment. Bye!"

FIRST REFLECTION:
"A MEETING PLACE WITH JESUS"

It is impossible to meet someone in the place you would like to be, if you are not actually there. It is impossible to meet someone in the place where you think you ought to be, if it is not a place where you can be. It is impossible to meet in the place where you were yesterday, if you are somewhere else today.

Jesus is actively seeking us out in this world. Each one of us. He wants to meet with us. He wants to invite us into an intimate relationship with him, with his Father, with the Holy Spirit. But imagine how difficult it is for Jesus to meet with us in the place where we were, where we would like to be, or where we think we ought to be, if we are not and cannot be there? Difficult? No: impossible. Not even God can meet us somewhere where we are not. He goes there. We don't show up. That's that.

But, of course, Jesus doesn't go there in the first place. He knows we are not there. Instead, Jesus always comes to us each day where we actually are. But we seldom look for him where we actually are, so we do not see him. We think we need to be somewhere else in order to meet with him. We are so full of notions about where we ought to be and want to be, that we are not prepared, or even open, to meet with him where we are, as we are.

When we look at the truth of who we really are, we may not like what we see. Our thoughts, feelings and actions often do not line up with the thoughts, feelings and actions of the person we like to think we are, or the person we want to be, or know we ought to be! We end up living with a kind of "identity through wishful thinking"! When we live our life pretending to be the person we ought to be, we relegate our real self to the realm of the unacceptable.

Suppose I have what I consider to be an ugly feeling: my friend gets a promotion at work and I feel resentful. I believe that I 'shouldn't' feel what I am actually feeling, because I believe that the person I 'ought' to be would never feel that way.

I'm so appalled at my real feelings, actions and thoughts that I refuse to acknowledge their existence. They're *un*-Christian. I'm a Christian. But there is a growing contempt in me . . . for me. And I'm living in fear that others will see through the disguise.

On top of this, I tend to assume that God feels and thinks about me exactly as I do. God is shocked by what I feel and think and do. I suspect that the real person I am revolts him. He would never meet with me as I really am. God is far too clean to tolerate being anywhere near my dirt.

There is some of this pattern in most of us: we run from who we are and seek escape into fantasies about the person we think we should be, or we want to be, or hope to be some day. This cardboard cut-out version—our fantasy—is the person we tend to present to God in prayer. As a result, prayer does not seem very real and it certainly does not touch our life very deeply. We are frustrated: we do not seem to be getting any closer to God.

This life of disconnection from the real person we are can take on especially powerful dimensions in a church, where we may have the added pressure of trying to conform ourselves to notions of who a real Christian is—what an 'authentic Christian' would do, say, think, and feel. Instead of sharing the truth of who we are with others there, we share the truth of who we think we should be. Since we are probably not alone in this pathetic enterprise, there is little depth or genuineness to our relationships. This is seldom a conscious program of deception. We are so intent upon trying to project an image of the person we want and/or ought to be that we seldom if ever notice the gap between the product as advertised and the product itself. We begin to believe that we are what we advertise.

One consequence of this condition—perhaps the most devastating—is the loss of the possibility of intimacy. The deep sharing of who we are that is the basis of intimacy is critically undermined when we withhold so much of ourselves—our real but "unacceptable" selves—from other people. But we also withhold our real but unacceptable selves from God. As a result, our spiritual life in particular becomes a great unsolvable puzzle. We do not understand this thing that keeps happening to us all the time: we make so many appointments with Jesus, but have so few meetings.

We need to be clear: it is OK and even important to know the kind of person God desires, and empowers us to become. But learning a lot about that person does not, in itself, cause us to become that person. It is OK and even important for us to see the sin and brokenness in us and to become convinced of and committed to the fulfillment of our call to become, by God's grace, the person we can be. But these good things do not in themselves cause us to be the person God calls us to be.

We become the persons we were created to be by allowing Jesus to meet us in the truth of who we are. There we come to see ourselves with his eyes. And only there do we begin to know him. I repeat: we cannot skip out on that meeting if we want to know Jesus.

You cannot experience the truth of Jesus without being willing to experience the truth of you. You cannot be in the place where Jesus is unless you are willing to be in the real place where you are. He has come very near to you where you are, as you are—that is where he is to be found.

The 'way' that Jesus has opened up for all of us is a path upon which we move, with him, from where we really are to the place where he has made it possible for us to be: home again, with the One who made us: with our heavenly Father.

So the reality of Jesus meeting with us is ugly and beautiful. On the one hand, we do not live up to our press releases—we are not the person we tried to be. We have been deceptive. We have been deceived. This is the ugly part. But, on the other hand, he loves us exactly as we are. This is the beautiful part.

Just being ourselves with Jesus means we can stop playing games. It means we can get off the stage where we are acting—out of this stuffy and restrictive costume. It means we can step out of the illusions about who we are. Instead of trying to maintain them, we endure the pain (sometimes the joy!) of seeing the truth, because we want the meeting more than we want feelings of familiarity and comfort. We come to see that meeting as life itself. And it is.

If we were to come to Jesus as we are, seeking to meet him as he is, we would find ourselves meeting with him in the place of truth: the foot of the cross.

As we begin to meet there with Jesus, the power of his obedient death begins to work in us. We experience the truth that he was crucified for our sake, so that we can suffer the death of all that is killing us!

What wonderful benefits there are for us in this dying! That scandalous cross becomes the place where we come to know the wonder and the joy of being our Father's child. There is no better thing! But we are able to know who we are only because that place of meeting is the place where our false self is put to death. From the cross Jesus tells us the truth about who we are: sinners so loved by God.

The cross of Christ becomes the place where we know the benefits of the unimaginable depths of his forgiveness, precisely because it is also the place where the depth of our sin is revealed. We see the ironic truth that though he died once for all, we continue to crucify him day by day.

The place of truthful meeting with Jesus becomes the place where light begins to fill our eyes and we see his beauty. He gives sight to those born blind. Our vision is restored and brought back again and again to the truth of what the Father has done for love of us. The beauty of his love is seen there in the depths of the suffering of his Son.

It is the Father who embraces us, in his Son, from the hard wood of the cross. As we yield to his loving embrace, death is put to death in us! And then, on the other side of the cross, as we are raised up by his Spirit, in his Son, we come to know the overwhelming joy of truth-filled life. We live there in intimacy with the God who loves us as we are, and who, in the embrace of that love, creates us anew.

But we cannot have the life God the Father wants us to have unless we are willing to make appointments with Jesus in places where we actually are. It is only there, in the place where we are lost, that he meets us as Savior.

When we are with him there, as we are, a veil is removed from our hearts and we know the truth: Jesus loves the place where we are more than all the bright and beautiful lands where we would like to be, or where we think we ought to be, or where we think we need to be in order to earn his love.

Because Jesus loves you as you are, he loves meeting with you as you are. You too will come to love the truth of who you really are more than anything else, because that truth is the place of meeting with him. Instead of spending time trying to distract and misdirect him, you will be spending time discovering new and more effective ways of meeting with him there in the truth of you.

Because Jesus and the Father and the Holy Spirit are there, the place where you are together is holy ground. Come as you are. And have no fear. He never misses a meeting when it's at your place, there at foot of the cross.

First Reflection In A Nutshell
"A Meeting Place with Jesus"

This scene and reflection centered on the impossibility of meeting with anyone, especially with God, in any place other than the very real place where we actually are. We explored some of the profound benefits of meeting with Jesus in the simple truth of what we think and feel.

Questions for reflection or discussion

1. What part of a typical day are you least likely to view as an opportunity to meet with Jesus? Ask him to be with you in that very place/time every day. Ask him for the grace to see and hear him there/then.

2. Do you sometimes completely ignore what you really feel or think because it is not what you believe you "ought" to feel or think? Do you ever condemn yourself, accuse yourself, or call yourself names when you have thoughts or feeling which you believe you should not have? Would acknowledging those thoughts/feelings and opening them to Jesus *as they occur* be the same thing as "giving them power"?

3. Is there anything you believe you know about yourself that you have never shared with Jesus? Share it with him now. Release it to him. Listen with your heart to his heart. Yield your mind to his understanding of you.

4. "You cannot experience the truth of Jesus without being willing to experience the truth of you." Do you believe this? If so, why and how is it true? If not, would there be a way of "testing it out" in real life? Would you be willing to ask Jesus about it?

5. Is it difficult for you to believe that Jesus loves you exactly where and as you are? Why? Why not?

MEDITATION ON PSALM 16
". . . O Lord, you are my portion and my cup . . . my boundaries enclose a pleasant land . . . ."

As I come to you, my refuge, I acknowledge this truth: I have been an enemy of your will for me. I have acknowledged and named and appeased false gods. I have tasted the bitterness and known the hollow emptiness.

The truth is that many things seemed good, but only you are good. The truth is that I drank from many foreign streams, but I am filled and sustained only by the cup you offer to me.

I have not always seen the value of the way you have opened for me. Your way has seemed very limiting. I have felt hemmed in. But I have come to know that within the boundaries you set, there is abundant life to be known and lived. When I accept your way and release myself to be within your protecting, directing word, I know a delight and fulfillment—a joy and peace unknown outside the confines of your will.

> Your boundaries open me up!
> Your walls are freedom!
> I enter your "narrow gate", Jesus.
> Obedience leads me to your right hand, Father,
> Then to your heart,
> Which is open and free: boundless,
> As only the place of perfect love can be.

SCRIPTURAL SCENE:
"JESUS WITH MARY"

Luke 10:38-41

As Jesus and his disciples were on their way, he came to a village where a woman named Martha opened her home to him. She had a sister called Mary, who sat at the Lord's feet listening to what he said. But Martha was distracted by all the preparations that had to be made. She came to him and asked, "Lord, don't you care that my sister has left me to do the work by myself? Tell her to help me!" "Martha, Martha," the Lord answered, "you are worried and upset about many things, but only one thing is needed. Mary has chosen what is better, and it will not be taken away from her."

John 12:1-11

Six days before the Passover, Jesus arrived at Bethany, where Lazarus lived, whom Jesus had raised from the dead. Here a dinner was given in Jesus' honor. Martha served, while Lazarus was among those reclining at the table with him. Then Mary took about a pint of pure nard, an expensive perfume; she poured it on Jesus' feet and wiped his feet with her hair. And the house was filled with the fragrance of the perfume.

But one of his disciples, Judas Iscariot, who was later to betray him, objected, "Why wasn't this perfume sold and the money given to the poor? It was worth a year's wages." He did not say this because he cared about the poor but because he was a thief; as keeper of the money bag, he used to help himself to what was put into it. "Leave her alone," Jesus replied. "It was intended that she should save this perfume for the day of my burial. You will always have the poor among you, but you will not always have me."

SECOND REFLECTION:
"GIVING AND RECEIVING"

Mary, the sister of Lazarus and Martha, is a person who lived out a depth of faithfulness not surpassed in any of Jesus' followers, including the twelve. Her ways are the ways of intimacy, and her faithfulness is a model for our lives of devotion to Jesus. I believe we can see this most clearly in her willingness to enter into unreserved, extravagant giving and receiving with him.

We see her first when Jesus comes to the home of Martha and Mary, as described in Luke's Gospel. Mary has drawn close to Jesus, hungry for his word and hungry for closeness with him. She sits at his feet. She gives him all her attention and listens intently to all he has to say.

For Mary, Jesus was simply the best. There was no place better than near him, at his feet. There were no words in the world better than those with which he anointed her as she lifted her face to him.

I believe that Mary acted from a deep devotion of mind and heart. She loved Jesus by seeking to be with him. She loved him by valuing him more than anything or anyone else. She loved him by being open to the truth that he was, and by her quiet readiness to be washed by his word.

Having seen Mary express her devotion to Jesus by her faithful willingness to receive from him, we turn now to John's Gospel where we see her drawing close to Jesus. Again she is at his feet, but now she comes to give, not to receive.

She gives extravagantly from what she has as she pours out a pure and fragrant anointing. Having given what she has, she then gives something even more precious as she wipes his feet with her hair. In this act of devotion to him, she gives of herself. Having received the word he spoke and the word he was, Mary now gives Jesus what she has and who she is. Mary loved Jesus through her willingness both to receive from him and give to him. This is the language of intimacy.

In the same way, Jesus loves her in his giving and in his receiving. He gave to Mary in such a wonderfully personal way. Jesus, who understood perfectly the cost of extravagant love, gave to her first by honoring that same love in Mary.

He was with her as she paid the price for loving him. First her sister and then the disciple try to heap condemnation and a large load of guilt on her. In the first instance because she had received. In the second because she had given.

First, Mary risked censure because she wanted to be close to Jesus and learn from him. He inspired in her the desire for something more, for what was best: for him! And when she responded, Jesus gave her a great gift. He honored the desire of her heart. Far from supporting the censure of her sister Martha, Jesus gave to Mary by counting her fully worthy to learn from him. He gave to her by receiving her.

In John's Gospel Mary gives a gift of tender devotion to Jesus. She lavishes an expensive ointment on him, simply because he is so precious that the value of the nard is nothing compared to the treasure he is to her. And Jesus receives her gift extravagantly. Far from supporting the censure of Judas, he honors and affirms her act of love, and invests it with a profound significance beyond anything that could have been intended by Mary. Jesus receives Mary's gift with such largeness of heart and mind that the receiving itself becomes a gift. This is perhaps the greatest gift.

In all of this, Mary enters into a relationship with Jesus that is the one he calls each of us to. This relationship with Jesus is one of intimacy, characterized by the giving and receiving of precious gifts—gifts of what we have and of who we are. We receive and we give. But those things become possible for us only because our precious Lord has given himself to us and received us first.

He pays the cost of uncommon love and anoints us with his word; with his presence; with his life. As we offer our new life to him, he invests it with more significance than we do. More than we could have hoped for.

Because Jesus has poured out his extravagant love, we can know the joy of accepting the gift of his acceptance, and the even greater joy of anointing him with the devotion of our lives.

Second Reflection In A Nutshell
"Giving and Receiving"

We have seen Mary, the sister of Lazarus and Martha, as the one who meets with Jesus in the place of devotion and intimacy. Their meetings illustrate the kind of mutual giving and receiving that is central to the deep connectedness of intimate relationship.

Questions for reflection or discussion

1. Mary suffers criticism and rebuke as she lives out her devotion to Jesus. Our desire to receive from or give to Jesus can provoke a hostile response from others, even friends and family. Have you witnessed or personally experienced this? Have you been the one with resentment?

2. Martha seems to feel that she is getting the raw end of the deal. Does Jesus disagree with her?

3. Do you believe that it could cost **you** something for *someone else* to live out her devotion to God? Considering the love Mary had for Jesus, is it possible that at times—especially at the foot of the cross—she "paid a price" for Jesus' devotion to the Father?

4. Jesus "gave to [Mary] by receiving her." What must you do to know the joy of receiving from Jesus in this way?

5. We give gifts of what we have and of who we are. Which do you find more difficult to give? To receive? Would your answers depend upon whether you were referring to God or to a human person?

MEDITATION ON PSALM 6
". . . The Lord has heard the sound of my weeping . . ."

With my weeping comes the truth,
Seeping then trickling,
Then in a flood, Lord.
Tears of hurt,
Tears of bitterness,
Tears of deep sadness,
Tears of anger, tears of loss,
Indignant tears, frustration tears;
All, precious lover of my soul, become
Tears of truth mingling—
A rising flood of release.
I am carried out in this cleansing wave—
Out from the place of fear and shame.
You blessed my flooding tears with life.
There is no ark in sight; I flow
Deep in the current of this Kingdom flood
And my dry, aching bones are drenched
And my eyes are watered
And I see again.
I see you now,
You who have been my enemy.
I have wanted you gone.
Yes, go!
Go to your bed and weep.
May there be tears of truth.
May God's life rise in you!

SCRIPTURAL SCENE:
"JESUS WITH PETER AND JUDAS"

John 13:1-17

It was just before the Passover feast. Jesus knew that the time had come for him to leave this world and go to the Father. Having loved his own who were in the world, he now showed them the full extent of his love.

The evening meal was being served, and the devil had already prompted Judas Iscariot, son of Simon, to betray Jesus. Jesus knew that the Father had put all things under his power, and that he had come from God and was returning to God; so he got up from the meal, took off his outer clothing, and wrapped a towel around his waist. After that, he poured water into a basin and began to wash his disciples' feet, drying them with the towel that was wrapped around him.

He came to Simon Peter, who said to him, "Lord, are you going to wash my feet?"

Jesus replied, "You do not realize now what I am doing, but later you will understand."

"No," said Peter, "you shall never wash my feet."

Jesus answered, "Unless I wash you, you have no part with me."

"Then, Lord," Simon Peter replied, "not just my feet but my hands and my head as well!"

Jesus answered, "A person who has had a bath needs only to wash his feet; his whole body is clean. And you are clean, though not every one of you." For he knew who was going to betray him, and that was why he said not every one was clean.

When he had finished washing their feet, he put on his clothes and returned to his place. "Do you understand what I have done for you?" he asked them. "You call me 'Teacher' and 'Lord,' and rightly so, for that is what I am. Now that I, your Lord and Teacher, have washed your feet, you also should wash one another's feet. I have set you an example that you should do as I have done for you. I tell you the truth, no servant is greater than his master, nor is a messenger greater than the one who sent him. Now that you know these things, you will be blessed if you do them.

THIRD REFLECTION:
"FIRST YOU MUST RECEIVE"

The great English Bishop William Temple said this about love: "Love grows by the acts that express it." One of the implications of this is that there is no great love without great expressions of it.

So what would it mean if someone were to say, "I have so much love for you, but I just don't, and never have been able to, express it in any way." Well, for one thing it would mean that this is no great love we are talking about. There may be a lot of feelings, but there is confusion concerning both the origin and the object of the feelings.

Love is not a feeling—although love certainly must involve our feelings if it is to be like the love of God. Love is primarily an activity.

Love without expression is not love at all. Love is how we spend our lives . . . concretely. It is the investment of our energies of mind, body, and spirit. Because that is true, Jesus says that the greatest love is demonstrated in the person who invests it all: who lays down his life for a friend [John 15:13].

In Jesus, God has called us "friend." Jesus said, "I don't call you servants—servants don't know what their master is doing. But I call you friends" [John 15:15]. And he laid down his life for us, his friends." He goes even further: he lays down his life for his enemies. He dies for those weeping at his feet *and* for those dividing his garments.

This is the greatest expression of love ever because it is the greatest love ever expressed.

But Jesus matched the depth of the love expressed in his death with the quality of the love he expressed in his life. The life Jesus modelled for—and offered to—the disciples, is the highest, greatest form that human life can take: the life of a servant [Matthew 20:26b-28]. But why is that? What is the connection between Jesus coming among us as the incarnate Word of love from the Father, and his coming among us as a servant?

I believe that the life of service is the life of loving, because at the center of the love relationship is self-giving. This is demonstrated in the love between Jesus and his Father: their intimacy is rooted in a mutual love that withholds nothing one from the other. For Jesus, this self-giving love was most perfectly expressed in his obedience to his Father's commission to come among us, not robed in the power and glory that he had a right to claim, but clothed in humility . . . as one who serves [Philippians 2:6-8].

You may be sure that Peter thought he was ready to follow Jesus into that life of service. He would have washed Jesus' feet any time, anywhere. But he was horrified that Jesus would offer to wash his feet. Yet, that was exactly what was needed and Jesus knew it. Peter needed to learn humility.

For Peter—for us—humility does not begin with giving service, but with receiving it. When we first draw close to our Savior, it is to receive. Receiving humbles us. It can be much harder than giving. There can be a lot of pride in giving. It may be that we find a lot of satisfaction in performing our charitable acts on those less fortunate than we are. But it does not stretch us to reach down from above, clear about who has the needs. Our serving can be full of subtle pride when we have not first learned humility.

Without that learning we act like a servant, but it's an act.

The highest form of human life is not found in the one who acts like a servant, but rather in the one who *is* a servant. Peter needed to receive the ministry that Jesus offered, or all that he did afterward would have been a denial of Jesus' life. No matter what he looked like to the world, he would have been a counterfeit servant. He needed washing by the only perfectly humble man who ever lived. Before he could give, he would have to learn how to receive.

We need what Peter needed. If we try to give without having received, more often than not our giving simply functions as another way of getting. All the outward "doing" can function as a way of distracting ourselves from the mess inside us that has not been submitted to the servant ministry of Jesus Christ.

Later, Jesus would call Peter to give away the love that Jesus had given him [John 21:15-17]. But Peter would never have been able to give away that love if he had been unwilling to receive it first. This receiving had to be personal and risky. Being around Jesus was not enough.

Judas was with Jesus every day. Judas heard all the words. He saw the deeds. He went out with Jesus to do acts of service. But did he receive from him?

Here is an amazing thing to consider: apparently Judas had his feet washed by the Son of God! But it wasn't enough. His heart wasn't open. He didn't receive on the inside what was offered on the outside. He was dirty even after Jesus had washed his feet. He did the outward things—things that looked as though he was allowing Jesus to make him clean. But on the inside he was in rebellion.

Judas did not open himself and become vulnerable to the cleansing presence of Jesus Christ. He thought he was taken care of already. He thought he was in control. He had made his plans. They did not include being humbled or served.

He did not know that the death Jesus was about to suffer was for *him*: the expression of a love so great that it could defeat death, and pride, and betrayal. Judas did not know who he was—did not know he was so loved by God.

But Jesus washed the feet of the one he knew would betray him. There was never a more humble act. He could do it because, unlike Judas, Jesus knew who he was. He knew where he had come from, what he was doing here, and where he was going [John 13:3].

He had lived a life of perfect openness to receive all his Heavenly Father had to give him. The Father had washed his feet in the river Jordan. And as Jesus came up out of the water, his Father had washed him with words of love . . . "This is my Beloved Son . . . ." It was the perfect love they share that Jesus expressed when he laid down his life for us. Jesus expresses his love for the Father by loving us. His love is expressed in his obedience. His obedience is expressed in his servant ministry among us.

We are his friends. If we allow him, he will wash our feet. This looks like submitting ourselves to healing in the places of hurt in our lives. It looks like repenting of our sin, turning from it and receiving his forgiveness.

He wants to make us whole. He came to make us clean. He humbled himself to teach us humility. He died to give us the life he wants to pour out for the world. He will make it possible for us to become servants who know who they are, where they have come from, what they are doing here, and where they are going.

By his grace we can be as humble as Peter became.

Jesus answered, "Unless I wash you, you have no part with me." "Then, Lord," Simon Peter replied, "not just my feet but my hands and my head as well!"

When he saw what was at stake, he wanted to be the most humble man alive. He wanted to be deluged with receiving!

It's kind of funny. It's kind of wonderful.

He could have taken the path Judas took. Peter, in his own way, betrayed Jesus too. But Peter was saved, in part, by his willingness to accept all the benefits of the love of God. He allowed Jesus to wash him inside and out. Later, he received cleansing forgiveness from the Risen Lord [John 21:15-19]. And new life. The life of a servant.

Third Reflection In A Nutshell
"First You Must Receive"

This scene and reflection has explored the foundation of our ability to give. We must receive from Jesus before we can enter into his life of self-giving love for others.

Questions for reflection or discussion

1. "Love grows by the acts that express it," says Bishop William Temple. Would your love for God grow if you were to find new ways to express your love? What about your love for other people?

2. Do you believe it is possible that one might "act like a servant" and yet not truly "be a servant"?

3. Have you allowed Jesus to "wash your feet"? What connection, if any, do you see between that experience and humbleness in you? If you had to name the single most important characteristic of a humble heart, what would it be?

4. Jesus "knew who he was . . . where he had come from . . . what he was doing here and where he was going." What do you think is the connection between that and his ability and willingness to wash "the feet of the one he knew would betray him"?

5. ". . . Whoever wants to become great among you must be your servant, and whoever wants to be first must be your slave . . . ." [Matthew 20:26b-27a]. Jesus seems to be saying that a desire to be "great" (in the kingdom of God) is not at odds with a desire to be humble. Is there resistance in you to asking Jesus to make you "great"? If you were to ask that of Jesus, would you be declaring anything more than your desire to be like him? Does the desire to be insignificant in the kingdom of God come from a humble heart?

PRAYING THE SCRIPTURE, PART 1
"I will not leave you orphans; I will come to you."

Thank you, Jesus, for this word—your word—which comes to me in every kind of circumstance. Even when I cannot feel your presence I am embraced by your steadfast word—your promise. Because of your word of assurance, even the hardest of times can simply be a season when I wait expectantly for you.

Give me the grace, Father, to reach out for your gifts—always just right for this particular day.

For the grace to hope steadily, thank you. I receive your hope into every nagging doubt; into every chamber where a condemning word is whispered. I receive you when I feel like an orphan, abandoned and alone.

For your peace, which frees me to enter restfully and fruitfully into every season, thank you. I receive your peace in the pit of my stomach, into the small of my back, into my hands, open and ready, into my heart where I have experienced you coming so many times to dispel my fear.

Thank you for drawing my mind into my Father's creative mind. Thank you for the grace to focus not so much on what I do not seem to have, but on all that is of you—on the radiant beauty of all that you have made.

Thank you for eyes to see the sin I continue to choose, which causes me to walk sadly away from your presence.

I receive with thanksgiving all that you reveal to me in this day, precious Jesus.

Thank you, Jesus, that you came to me and loved me first. You did not meet me halfway; it was you who journeyed. Before I knew the object of my yearning—before I had the grace to choose you, or offer myself to you, you fulfilled a promise unknown to me. Before I woke to light you came as light. Before I had eyes to see you, you saw me and loved me and came to me as truth. For this freedom to *see* and to *be*, thank you Jesus.

Come, Lord Jesus!

C hapter Two

INTIMACY:
A place where the word of love makes us new

The intimacy now possible in Jesus Christ is like that intimacy known in the depth of communion between a perfectly loving parent and child. Chapter 2 focuses on our fulfillment as adopted sons and daughters of our heavenly Father.

SCENE: "I CAN'T THANK YOU ENOUGH!"

["She", a young woman in her early thirties, is sitting and talking at a table with a friend. Jesus, unseen, sits at the table with them. "She" is rejoicing with her friend over the changes she sees in herself. She is aware that her ability to receive and to give love is growing. She tells her friend that she is coming to accept God's love for her and is beginning to learn how to love herself.]

Friend: There *is* something different about you. Maybe there's hope for me. I feel like I just go around in circles—it's the same old stuff all the time.

She: Believe me, I know what you mean. I guess the thing that's different for me this time is that I'm beginning to know what I need. The truth is I've never liked myself and I've never really been able to accept everything they say about how God loves me. I know he loves others . . . but I've never believed he actually loves me. But I need to know his love and I'm choosing to be more open to it. He's actually getting through to me every once in a while. It's really happening! I'm beginning to . . .
["Slammer" enters quickly during last phrases. He slams a book down nearby, interrupting her.]

She: *[Visibly and audibly startled]* Is that you?

Slammer: Who do you think it is?

She: I wish you wouldn't do that; I'm nervous enough without you slamming things around just because you're frustrated. You never change! Some people need to grow up!

Slammer: Like who?

She: Who do you think?

Slammer: You're one to talk! You're the one who never changes. In fact I think you're worse than you were before all this talk about being different!

She: I can't believe you said that!

Slammer: I can't believe the way you say one thing and do another!

She: That's so judgmental!

Slammer: That's' so hypocritical!

She: Why don't you just slam your way out of here!

Slammer: Fine!

She: Great!

       [She turns to face her friend.]

Slammer: *[Out of sight]* Wonderful!

She: *[She turns back . . . then yells back into the empty air . . .]* Perfect!
       [She faces her friend once more; composes herself; remembers her topic.]

She: Anyway! The point is that God's love really is beginning to grow in me. And because of that I'm actually starting to love myself for the first . . .

       [During the preceding, a look of shock and shame comes over her and she hides her face in her hands . . . .]

Friend: Don't let him get to you. *[Begins to reach out as though to comfort her, but, instead, looks at her watch.]* Listen—I have to go, but we'll talk real soon. OK?

She: *[Almost inaudibly . . . face still in her hands]* OK.

       ["Friend" leaves quietly]

Jesus: You really are growing in my love.

She: *[Not looking at Jesus]* How can you say that?

Jesus: Just a few months ago, that wouldn't have bothered you the way it's bothering you now.

She: *[She lifts her face.]* That's true.

Jesus: You'd have nursed your anger for hours.

She: True.

Jesus: For days.

She: True.

Jesus: For weeks.

She: *[Pause . . . then soft laughter]* True.

Jesus: Things are going to seem worse for a while, but don't give up: I'm just answering your prayer.

She: What prayer?

Jesus: You asked me to show you your heart.

She: *[With gentle irony]* I *can't* thank you enough!

Jesus: You're *too* welcome!

       [She smiles]

Jesus: I love you.

She: *[Very differently than before]* I can't thank you enough.

FIRST REFLECTION:
"ACCEPTING THE UNACCEPTABLE"

On the road to new life with God—a life of close communion—we begin with acceptance or we do not really begin at all. That, of course, means God's acceptance of us, *as we are*. His acceptance of us makes our acceptance of us possible. The path where Jesus finds us, however, is the one where we are trying to become acceptable to God. Much of the time we act as though we believe we can accomplish it, with just a bit more effort (starting tomorrow). Once we become acceptable, then God will love us—really love us for who we are: acceptable! Finally! We suspect that the only alternative is God's toleration. Oh, he will 'love' us, of course, after his fashion, because, after all, he is God and he has to.

It is important to acknowledge that there is truth to our worst fear: we are not acceptable. This is the problem: there is absolutely nothing we can do to make ourselves acceptable. The spiritual task is as impossible as the physical task of trying, literally, to pick yourself up by your own "bootstraps". If you are hungry for a clear, comic lesson in absurdity, try it. Physical laws defeat all the eye-popping effort we can muster. Yet we are continually trying to accomplish the spiritual equivalent. The whole pathetic enterprise cannot stand the light of day. Our illusions fade quickly as soon as we shine even the faintest rays of honesty or truth on them. There, in the light, we see that we have struggled against spiritual laws that cannot be moved.

We must not be ignorant of another truth: we are not alone in our efforts. Satan is right behind the notion that we can and must continue to try to lift ourselves up into acceptability by our own efforts. All our striving simply provides opportunity after opportunity for judgment and condemnation: the truth that we are not acceptable comes to us by a variety of means in the ordinary course of our day and that truth serves to condemn us.

But how is it that a truth can lead to condemnation? There are two ways. First, when it is not spoken in love. Most of us have experienced this many times. We have heard something true about us spoken from a heart of revenge, condemnation, or jealousy. Far from coming as light—far from setting us free—it brings us under the weight of judgment. Very few people can make constructive, creative use of truth when it comes as a weapon that wounds.

It should be noted that before we walk in God's acceptance and love, we continually condemn *ourselves* with the truth.

Second, if a truth which is not the whole truth is *presented* as the whole truth, it becomes a lie. For example, let us suppose that I am engaged. A single woman I find attractive asks me if I am married. I give her my most engaging smile and say, "Me? Absolutely not!" An *internal* dialogue begins.

"Hmm." [*My conscience rumbles and wrinkles its forehead.*]

"Well, it *is true*, isn't it?"

"Hmm."

"Really! I'm *not* married! Not yet!"

"Yes, but your 'truth' is well on the way to functioning as a lie. It is true, but it was presented as the whole truth, and it is not the *whole* truth. Is it?"

"Well . . . ."

"Is it?"

"Well . . . I suppose . . . ."

"That's better. Stop thinking. Tell her the whole truth."

"Oh, well . . . alright . . . fine!"

How does this work in our struggle with acceptance? It may come in a thought: "Look at your life! There's no way you are acceptable to a holy and righteous God." The potentially destructive power in this thought comes from its plausibility. The truth of my sinfulness is apparent. My sin can never be acceptable to God. But the judgment and condemnation in me is nourished by this truth when it stands alone and I see nothing else. In that narrow world, the Savior has not come. I am not looking at the whole truth. I fail to take into account the fact that the Savior has come!

The fuller truth is that when I was an unrepentant sinner, when I was in open rebellion and completely unacceptable, Jesus died for me. For merciful love of me. In doing this he was demonstrating the Father's love for me as it really is.

The fuller truth is that there is no greater love than the love Jesus expressed by giving himself for unacceptable me. Since that is as far as you go in loving, how am I, by "becoming more acceptable", going to persuade God to love or accept me more? The truth is that he wants to give me the power to accept his acceptance and the grace to receive his love.

The fuller truth is that the Father does *love* each of us, but he does not accept us because of who *we* are, he accepts us because of who *Jesus* is! Jesus, by the Holy Spirit, pours out his acceptable life into us and offers his perfectly acceptable life to the Father, *for* us. The Father accepts the offer with perfect joy—it was his plan, after all! The Father is both just *and* the justifier [Romans 3:26]!

Feel *un*acceptable? Run, don't walk: flee to Jesus and hide yourself in him. That is where your acceptable life is hidden [Colossians 3:3].

To repeat, most of us have great difficulty receiving God's graceful acceptance. When the Holy Spirit comes with the Father's gift we are too busy trying to become acceptable. But there is more—a hidden agenda. It is not just that accepting his acceptance is *difficult* for us. The fact is that we do not *want* the acceptance God is offering. We are *offended* by the idea of any acceptance which is not based on our *acceptability*. We want to be accepted for our great merits and accomplishments. We certainly do not want to live a life which is based on unmerited acceptance *because that would put us under a debt that we can never repay.* And we do not want to live as debtors to anything, including mercy. We fear and resist what Robert Robinson celebrates in his great hymn about life in the Kingdom of God: *"O to grace how great a debtor daily I'm constrained to be."*

One consequence of our lack of self-acceptance, on the one hand, and our reluctance to yield our sinful lives to the mercy of God, on the other, is that we make even the smallest weight of sin into a crushing load. There are no simple sin pastries in the hellish kitchen of our judging hearts; we bake each sin or perceived failure into a poison-saturated, many layered cake. We serve this up until others run when they see us coming, and consume it ourselves until we are stuffed but starving.

Every perceived sin is evidence of my unacceptability. Each sin is evidence of my failure to do what I must do (be who I must be) in order to be acceptable. Very soon it is not my sin but my *response* to my sin that is the major problem.

Out of a reluctance to yield myself to the mercy of God, I have unwittingly chosen a life yielded to the mercy of me. And I have no mercy. I cannot afford any. After all, I am trying to become acceptable. Failure is not acceptable. Now I begin to mock and shame myself about failing. Then I am angry with myself for the mocking and the shaming. Now I really am beginning to have a problem. Pretty soon I am taking it out on you. Then I feel guilty about abusing you because I am angry for being ashamed that I have failed! Before I know it, I am bowed and broken under this crushing weight I have heaved up on to my own back. I have my poison layer-cake . . . and I am eating it too! "Who can rescue me from this body of death!" [Romans 7:24]

Praise be to God, who invites me to feed at the table of his loving acceptance! A wonderful truth opens up for me when I become a debtor to his mercy. I learn that the ultimate benefit of God's acceptance is not that I would learn to "cope" with all my sinfulness, and brokenness, and incompetence. Acceptance is only the beginning. As I step through that door, I come out into a land where grace makes profound change possible. The beginning of the Father's plan is acceptance, but its end is new birth into a relationship with the One who is Eternal Life.

The Father's plan unfolds in me only as I yield my life to God's merciful acceptance. As I become more and more a debtor to God's mercy, I become less and less a debtor to the judgment my sin brings on me from the outside and the inside. It becomes my desire to offer my sin up to him. It is not so much that I am trying to be good. I am just choosing to be my Father's child. That choice means yielding to him so that he can cleanse me, renew my mind with his word, recreate my heart with his love, and form me into the likeness of his Son.

As a debtor to God's mercy, I am not striving to fabricate or maintain my innocence. Rather, I am seeking to remain in the loving embrace of my Father, where his word of love tells me who I am. Because of what Jesus has done, I am not in panic or despair about what I have done. I am not trying to create or preserve my identity. I trust my Father to tell me who I am: his fully accepted, beloved child. And that identity does not depend upon anything I have *ever* done, but on my trusting acceptance of what my Father has done in his Beloved Son, Jesus, by his Spirit.

As a debtor to God's mercy, I am out of the business of trying to create a life I can offer that would be worthy of being received. I am about my Father's business, having received the gift of new life—of 'new creation'—he offers. As I am in him, I find that the Father's acceptance and love are one in me. The *whole truth* of that sets me free to accept and love myself as his child.

First Reflection In A Nutshell
"Accepting the Unacceptable"

God the Father pours out his love and mercy in the place where we are busy trying to become acceptable. In and through Jesus we are met by the whole truth of the Father's love for us and by the truth about our resistance to his mercy. He makes available to us the grace to accept his acceptance. As we receive God's Word of love we come out from under the weight of judgment and into deeper and deeper debt to his mercy and grace.

Questions for reflection or discussion

1. This reflection emphasizes the ironic truth that God accepts us as we are but not because we are acceptable. Reflect on this 'ironic truth' in the light of the difference between God's *acceptance of us as we are* and God's *approval of what we do*.

2. "God may accept me, but I never will!" How would such an attitude affect our relationship with God? With ourselves and/or with others?

3. Have you experienced truth being spoken to you without love? Did you experience that 'truth' as condemnation? Would it be possible to receive the truth without receiving the condemnation? Would that be desirable? What would make it possible?

4. "When a truth which is not the whole truth is presented as the whole truth, it becomes a lie." How common do you think this kind of 'lying' is in ordinary, everyday life? What might be the possible motivations for our lying in this way?

5. ". . . it is not my sin but my response to my sin that is the major problem." Given the fact that we do sin, what would be an alternative to the response that is like "a poison-saturated, many layered-cake"?

6. Are you in debt to God's mercy? Does that seem like a "good" thing to you? Would you want that debt to grow? Why? What would cause that debt to grow?

MEDITATION ON PSALM 8
"Out of the mouths of infants and children your majesty is praised above the heavens!"

What does your glory embrace, awesome God?
All that is!
All I can see and touch and
So much that I know nothing of!
Your creating, blessing hands
Gather even the heavens to your heart.
(All of it, Lord of Majesty, no more to you
Than a single small child held close;
And no less.)

In the midst of your glory I lose my mind.
I am shattered by even this dim awareness
Of the vast glory of what you have created,
And I am stunned by the truth
That you seek me out.
You entrust to me—your rebellious child—
The gentle whale and the fierce beetle.
Why? Why, Lord?
As I accept the truth of my revolt,
The question grows;
The wonder grows;
Praise forms;
I am faced squarely, roundly, with the truth
Of your scandalous pursuit and embrace.

Only a child can receive
This tender caring—
This honor—
This glory.
This child (too weak to lift to you a heavy question),
Your child, gives you what he has:
I praise your great name—
Your sweet great name.
You! Lord of Glory, I praise You!

SCRIPTURAL SCENE:
"JESUS WITH JOHN AND MARY"

John 19:25-27

Near the cross of Jesus stood his mother, and his mother's sister, Mary the wife of Clopas, and Mary Magdalene. When Jesus saw his mother there, and the disciple whom he loved standing nearby, he said to his mother, "Dear woman, here is your son," and to the disciple, "Here is your mother!" From that time on, this disciple took her to his home.

SECOND REFLECTION:
"A WORD OF LOVE"

God our Father has a word of love for us. He entrusts that word to Jesus. In fact, God's word of love to us was and *is* Jesus. One beautiful implication is this: as Jesus releases the Father's Word into this world, he gives himself away. He gives himself to us. Let's look at one way in which this self-giving might be experienced.

Perhaps you have been reading Psalm 139, and the last verses touch your heart and you begin to pray, "Lord, show me what is in my heart!" Then, a few days later, in some quiet time of prayer, Jesus comes as "The Truth" to you. At first you have no idea that that is what is happening. You are preoccupied, in this time of prayer, with something frustrating and upsetting that has happened between you and a friend. Suddenly you see your heart laid bare—you see jealousy or pettiness there in the way you behaved. Perhaps, like many people, seeing something like this in yourself brings feelings of shame, quickly followed by a whole courtroom full of legal proceedings, with you as the prosecuting attorney, the defendant, and the judge. The evidence is irrefutable. Condemnation follows. Sentence is pronounced: "Two days of bitter self-loathing! Next!"

But this time you notice a difference. The beginnings of shame are quickly overshadowed by a sense of melting—of mercy. You feel as though you are seeing yourself with new eyes. Not with the eyes of a judge, but with the eyes of mercy and love. The truth is the same, but you are not seeing that truth alone. Jesus is there with you. He does not fling truth at you from a distance. He is not presenting evidence. He draws very near to you in order to share something with you he sees which concerns him. He brings this to you personally because he loves you. He cares deeply about what goes on in you, and between you and your friend.

Incredibly, you are as aware of his love as you are of the jealousy you have seen in your heart! Somehow, they have become one. How can this be? It can be because his love entered in through the truth he shared. And the truth entered in through the love he shared. He met you there in the shame and the hidden longings of your heart. He spoke the "truth, in love". In releasing this word of loving truth within you, Jesus was giving himself away.

This self-giving flows from, and is a hallmark of, the love Jesus shares with his Abba. In fact, this word of love Jesus brings to us is, at its core, a word about the love between the Father and the Son. It is this love that the Holy Spirit pours out into our hearts. In this giving the Holy Spirit gives himself away.

The Lord of Glory has no gifts to give us that are not also gifts of his very being. Every gift he gives is personal—a gift of himself. God's love, for example, is not an object or a commodity. He does not hold love in his hand to be dispensed according to his will. He does not possess love, he is love [1John 4:8].

But how can it be that God *is* love? We know that love does not exist in the abstract, but only in, and as, a living relationship. The word has no meaning apart from personal relationship. How, then, can God *be* love? God can only be love if God is a relationship of love! And this, in fact, is the truth—known only in Jesus Christ by the Holy Spirit: God is love (and the source of all love) because *God is the divine relationship* of "persons," among whom perfect love is shared.

Love, therefore, is the intimate, perfectly loving relationship between the Father and the Son. It is this love that the Holy Spirit pours into our hearts. But, being God, the Holy Spirit has no gift to give that is not also a gift of himself. And so it is that the Person of the Holy Spirit fills our hearts. No wonder our hearts cry "Abba": the Holy Spirit has brought the love the only begotten Son has for the Father, and the love the Father has for the Son, *into our hearts*!

We, in turn, are invited into the heart of that Love Relationship—that divine communion—who is the living God. We come in as adopted "sons", having been given, by Jesus, the Son of God, his relationship with the Father and having been received as sons and daughters by the Father, in his Son [Romans 8:15-16]. We are in him as Jesus is in him. And he is in us as he is in his Son. We give ourselves to him! He gives himself to us!

So we see that self-giving love is the Father's way and his will. For Jesus, doing his Father's will is food and drink and joy [John 4:34, etc.]. And Jesus loves us so much that he wants us to be fed as he is fed and to know his joy! As he walks with us as Savior, Lord, and friend, *he shares the nourishment and the joy of his giving with us!* He gives away the giving! For love of us and for the sake of joy, he shares his joy!

That is what was happening as he hung on the cross. In that place of self-giving, Jesus had a word of love for his mother. He entrusted that word to the beloved disciple, John: "Here is your mother." He was not just providing for his mother. He was sharing with John the joy of loving Mary. Jesus had a word of love for John. He entrusted that word to his mother: "Here is your son." Jesus was not just thinking of his beloved disciple and friend, he was sharing with his mother the joy of loving John.

These words to John and Mary are a miracle of self-giving love. Even in this hour of agony, Jesus is moved by compassion. Jesus is concerned to lay down his life for the whole world, but his great, universal and saving love is expressed in the intimate terms of his loving concern for these *particular* broken-hearted people who have come to the foot of the cross. He is making provision for their sorrow and for their joy!

Jesus was inviting John and Mary to enter into a relationship with the Word of God (himself) at the center. Jesus' love and care brought them together and their love for one another would always be lived out in the context of their love for him. Do you suppose that there was ever a moment in their relationship when it was just John and Mary? Could Mary have looked at John and not thought of Jesus? And would not Mary always bring Jesus to John's mind and heart? Could they ever be together without Jesus being present?

Jesus comes knocking at the door of every one of our relationships. If the Word of God is at the center of our lives, then the love we have for one another in centered on and lived in the context of the love we have for him. In Jesus, all our relationships are mediated. If we are together, then he is present in the very heart of our togetherness. It is his love that we share. We know the greatest intimacy when we share in him.

As John and Mary entered into a new relationship, their identity as persons was shaped by their having known Jesus. They knew something about giving: they had received from the greatest giver who ever lived! Their capacity to be mother and friend and son for one another was transformed by the one who had given himself first as son and friend and master.

These words of love for John and Mary are the same words of love that Jesus speaks to us. God's self-giving love unites us in one Body—all the parts belonging deeply to the others—all loved into life: the one Body of those who know Jesus Christ as the living word of love who embraces us, inhabits our relationships and invites us to drink from the cup of self-giving—to be fed as he is fed!

And what scope there is for doing the Father's will! God has spoken a word of love to every sinful and broken person in this sinful and broken world, and God has entrusted that word to his Body, the Church, and to each of its members: "Beloved disciples . . . friends: there are your brothers and sisters; there is your mother and your father, your son and your daughter."

Jesus invites and empowers us to enter into his love for others. He invites me to share in his love for you and he invites you to share in his love for me. This is an invitation to do the will of our Abba, to be fed by the obedience of love, and to know the joy of giving ourselves away!

Second Reflection In A Nutshell
"A word of Love"

Because the Holy Spirit gives himself to us, the love Jesus and the Father share becomes the love we have to give away. In this giving we are nourished as Jesus is: by doing the Father's will.

Questions for reflection or discussion

1. "[Jesus] does not fling truth at you from a distance. He is not presenting evidence . . . In releasing this word of loving truth within you, Jesus was giving himself away." Have you ever considered that an opportunity to hear and receive Jesus is an opportunity to hear and receive truth? Could we also say that an opportunity to hear and receive truth is an opportunity to hear and receive Jesus? If you truly believed this, how would your life change?

2. We have seen that God, being love, "is a divine relationship of 'persons', among whom perfect love is shared." Although not divine, are we—each of us—as human persons also 'a relationship'? Reflect on this in the light of God's desire to come and live in us. Would or could his being 'in me' change the way I relate to myself: my attitude about me, my thoughts and feelings about me, the way I treat myself every day, etc? What exactly am I doing when I invite Jesus "into my heart"?

3. Do you believe that the Father is empowering us to become persons who, in giving gifts, 'give ourselves away' as he does? What would this look like, in everyday life, in terms of observable behavior? What about in terms of things that cannot be seen?

4. What do you think Jesus meant when he said "My food . . . is to do the will of him who sent me and to finish his work" [John 4:34]?

5. "He gives away the giving! For love of us and for the sake of joy, he shares his joy!" The implication here is that the greatest joy comes not in receiving, but in giving—in self-giving. Is this what you believe? Do the priorities of your life reflect this belief? Would we have more experience of this if our love for others was actually Jesus' love for them, living and expressing itself (himself) in and through us?

MEDITATION ON PSALM 17
"Keep me as the apple of your eye;
Hide me under the shadow of your wings!"

After my thoroughly self-righteous review—after all my cries of innocence—it has come to this: "keep me as the apple of your eye." What I really want, what I really need is that you be as a father to me. Whose deeply loving gentleness is rooted in unassailable strength—the strength to be wounded willingly every day for my sake. Who looks on me and into me with perfect tenderness, and receives, and celebrates me, with me, as I am, and as your love assures me I will become.

After all my strutting and pleading—after all my protests of purity—it has come to this: "hide me under the shadow of your wings." What I really want, what I really need is that you would be as a mother to me. I am afraid and I need to be gathered in by your fierce mother's love. Drawn into the circle of your protection; swept close under your wing, simply because I am yours and for no other reason.

After all the words of my mouth, dear Lord, it has come to this: I am your child. It is only in the nearness of you that I am safe and sure and satisfied.

SCENE: "ISAIAH'S WITNESS AND HIS CHALLENGE"

Isaiah 50:4-9a

Isaiah, prophet of God, is near the city gate. He has been prophesying and after a brief, introspective silence, he is about to start again. Within earshot are some who are in awe of this strange, fierce, yet compassionate man. A few feel deep gratitude for words that have lifted them up from deep pits of hopelessness and despair. Others have come to mock him. They have called out in derision many times as he spoke. A few men of some power and influence have listened very carefully—they would bring accusations of heresy and treason against him, if they could.

Isaiah has been speaking for some time with great intensity and conviction, principally about the sins of Israel. He delivers judgment. He shouts unthinkable, God-sanctioned defeat and exile. He speaks bitterly of the adulterous disloyalty of a chosen people. Yet he pleads with the voice of God's tender desire for his nation-bride. He has paused, as though spent. His highly expressive face speaks of an inner listening. His eyes are shut as he begins again, but more softly.

"The Sovereign Lord has given me an instructed tongue, to know the word that sustains the weary."

The words are released slowly. There is an almost child-like quality about him now. This is not a voice pitched for prophecy. This is personal. He goes on, caressing each word with wonder, as one who shares the truth of a precious gift.

"He wakens me morning by morning, wakens my ear to listen like one being taught."

As he continues, his voice and expression cleanse his words of any hint of boasting. Isaiah begins to look from face to face—each phrase seeming to dawn on him just as he utters it—as though something of great importance is coming clear for the first time.

"The Sovereign Lord has opened my ears, and I have not been rebellious; I have not drawn back. I offered my back to those who beat me, my cheeks to those who pulled out my beard; I did not hide my face from mocking and spitting."

Suddenly Isaiah's words ring out with joy and triumph.

"Because the Sovereign Lord helps me, I will not be disgraced."

His voice is strong now—his eyes bright with tears.

"Therefore have I set my face like flint, and I know I will not be put to shame. He who vindicates me is near. Who then will bring charges against me?"

Shouts are heard:

"I will!"

"Fool!"

"Your *words* are going to convict you, Isaiah! You know it. You know you've gone too far!"

Now, as he releases these final words, he is facing those who try to shout him down.

"Let us face each other! Who is my accuser? Let him confront me!"

But as he speaks his eyes lift higher, he no longer addresses those around him. His words are witness and worship.

"It is the Sovereign Lord who helps me. Who is he that will condemn me?"

As he finishes, cries and shouts are heard; scoffing from some, praise to God from others; curses *and* blessings—all of it lost on Isaiah, whose face, streaming with tears, is lifted to the God of Israel.

THIRD REFLECTION:
"THE WORD OF ETERNAL LIFE"

Isaiah speaks words of encouragement to a weary people, to sustain them. His ability to do this is rooted in the sustaining work of God in him. But the relationships of Isaiah's life are not all about encouragement. He has known opposition, chiefly through bitter expressions of contempt and violent attempts at humiliation. They want to stop him from speaking God's word. Regardless, Isaiah is undefeated and this scene ends with a boldly assured challenge to his adversaries to meet him in court.

"Let us face each other! Who is my accuser? Let him confront me."

Why is Isaiah so confident? In part, his confidence is rooted in the basic orientation of his life.

"The Sovereign Lord has given me an instructed tongue, to know the word that sustains the weary."

Isaiah's purpose is to go out to those around him who are discouraged and beaten down. He tells us later that he has set his face like flint. Toward what? Isaiah has his face set toward God, who, it is clear, orients him toward other people. He will not be moved from his call to bring to them the strengthening, life-restoring word that comes from God. If he unmasks sin and speaks of coming destruction, it is so that, seeing the truth, the nation may repent.

Isaiah's confidence comes in the face of attacks on him physically, mentally, and spiritually. If Isaiah were oriented toward preserving *Isaiah*, then these attacks might very well succeed in, as he says, 'confounding' him.

If one is on the path of self-preservation, then personal attacks are a threat to the direction, progress, and meaning of your life. But Isaiah is on another path, and attacks on him are no lasting threat to his progress on that path. He walks the way of a servant of God sent out to others.

When contempt comes his way, it may hurt, but it does not dissuade him from his course because he is not in the business of protecting his reputation or of maintaining his status in other people's eyes. He is free to continue on God's way. There is no place in him to receive the contempt. There is no room because he is filled right up with words God has given him for the people.

When he finds himself on the receiving end of violent acts whose purpose is to humiliate him—when he's attacked and beaten—it may hurt him, but it doesn't stop him. He is, as Paul says of himself in J.B. Phillips' wonderful paraphrase, "knocked down, but not out!" He just goes on with a sore back, less hair in his beard, and a cleaner face where the spit has been wiped away.

There is no insecure place in him making him vulnerable to the destructive power of judgment and shame. This is because he walks strong in the approval of God and secure in the experience of God's constant care for him. Isaiah puts it simply: "The Lord God helps me!" As a result, God's sustaining word through Isaiah to others has the authentic ring of words that can only come from one who, because he has experienced it, understands God's faithful provision.

God has equipped him for his going out with the ability to be among those to whom he is sent in ways that reach them and accomplish the divine purpose: he is inspired and competent. God has given him eyes to see the people exactly as they are and words to meet them exactly where they live. Isaiah needs no other provision on his path. And so Isaiah knows a confidence rooted in God's proven reliability. God leads him out and he is sure that God is behind him too.

So he issues his challenge to the opposition. "Come on, bring your contempt. We'll go to court. I'll meet you at the gate! You think the judge is going to rule in your favour? Well, you can think whatever you like, but I *know!*"

Here we come to it: in the deepest place Isaiah's confidence is founded on the fact that he knows something that his adversaries do not. Isaiah has inside information. You bet he's confident: *he knows the judge!*

He knows that the judge hearing the case is going to be the very same one who is there with him "morning by morning"! The judge is his sustainer! The judge is his helper!

The judge gave Isaiah the very words that offend his enemies! Their efforts to stop *Isaiah* from speaking are viewed by the Judge as an attempt to shut *his* mouth!

Isaiah's confidence is our own. We know the judge. He is the same one who wakens us to his truth and his love morning by morning. We do not have to fear that at the judgment hour, the judge is going to be switched on us and we will get someone we do not know. It is not going to be like that. The one with whom we walk day by day is to be our judge. We will be judged by the living Word who has come very near to us; by the Word who is transforming our minds and hearts. The One before whom we will stand on the last morning, will be the same mighty God by whose strength we stood yesterday; in whose embrace we live today; by whose word we will be fed tomorrow.

His verdict in that hour will not be "Guilty"! Nor will his verdict be "innocent"! He will look deeply into us and his verdict will be a word that meets us as Eternal Life. He will say: "I know you! You are my son! You are my daughter!" And that will be enough. And we will be satisfied. And his joy will be complete.

Third Reflection In A Nutshell
"The Word of Eternal Life"

In this scene and reflection we observe that Isaiah knows pain and the grief of opposition, but that he also knows the provision and faithfulness of God. God's word is with him and in him each day. His secret is our secret. His confidence is ours: we know the judge—it is he who wakens us to his truth and love morning by morning, who speaks the word of life, who tells us who we are.

Questions for reflection or discussion

1. "[Isaiah] walks the way of a servant of God sent out to others." How important was it for Isaiah to know with certainty that he was sent by God, when it came to withstanding opposition?
2. Isaiah was able to "walk strong in the approval of God." Based on this scriptural scene, what do you think it was about Isaiah that would have met with God's approval? In our lives, if we live in ways that meet with God's approval, how does that relate to our ability to live without vulnerability to discouragement and judgment from others?
3. "The Lord God helps me!", says Isaiah. What do you think would be the *fruit,* in your heart and in your life, of a strong, daily awareness of God's faithfulness to you?
4. Invite Jesus to be with you as you imagine yourself in a courtroom coming before a judge on a serious charge. You are rigid with fear. There is no jury: this judge will decide the case. He has all authority. You look up and see that you know the Judge: he is your father. You know his heart is full of love for you. He has "laid down his life" for you many times, in many ways, since you were born. Never was there a wiser, more merciful, compassionate, loving, forgiving man. He knows you completely and yet you know that he loves you unconditionally—without limit or reservation. He has been there for you all your life. He has taken you into his

arms. He has soothed your hurts. He always has time for you. Your joy is his: you have played and laughed together. He shares your pain: he has wept with you. Now look into his eyes. What do you see? Listen. What does he say? Watch. What does he do? Be with Jesus there.

PRAYING THE SCRIPTURE, PART 2
*"Before long the world will not see me anymore,
but you will see me."*

It is strange and wonderful, Jesus, that you went away in order to come closer. There are many things of this world to which I must say goodbye in order to come closer to you. You know how hard this is for me. It was no easier for you. But loving this world never kept you from seeing the Father. You yielded to your Father everything you saw; everything you heard and smelled and tasted and touched. I yield to you the world in me. I yield to you the eyes of the world in me. Give me your eyes.

Your promise stirs yearning in me: I want to see everything of my Father's Kingdom more clearly. I want to see you more clearly. I want to see the whole truth of who I am to you. I want to see your way each day. I want to see the turnings that bring me more fully into your life.

I thank you for these desires—I believe they are a gift from your heart to mine. I ask for the grace that these desires may be fulfilled at the cost of the death, in me, of all competing desires. Rise up before me, Lord, in each moment of choosing. Lift my eyes to you so that I may see and follow you. Be light to my eyes, Jesus, so that my body may be filled with your life—with every good and perfect gift from my Father's hand.

Thank you Jesus.

*C*hapter Three

INTIMACY:
A Place Of Trust

Trust is the doorway into a life of intimacy with God. This is a life that can only be lived by "faith." Trust is that aspect of faith which brings us into the place of God's grace.

SCENE: "THE FLY"

Note: It was 1974. My wife, Jude, and I were living in Indiana. I was in the middle of fishing around for focus in my life—struggling hard with my ambitions, with the realities of being newly married—trying to grope my way through an active life as a musician.

One day I was sitting around, minding my own business, when I suddenly became aware that there was a fly at one of the dining room windows, making a lot of noise. I went over and let him out. That sounds simple, but it wasn't. And it was far from easy. In fact it was a pretty intense experience getting him out of the house. When it was over, I was resting—trying to get my breath back—when something happened to me.

I could feel my face getting hot and flushed, but my mind became cool and my thoughts crystal clear. I felt a surge of adrenaline go through me—at least I thought that was what it was—it was like an electric current. The whole experience with the fly came back to me in one flash. I had the almost irresistible urge to write down what I was seeing and understanding. As I did, my whole perspective changed and I relived the event as a parable, full of humor and deep significance. Here is what I wrote that day so many years ago.

The Fly

There was a fly battering himself against my window this morning. He was on the inside, but from all indications I understood that it was his desire to get out. So, I opened the window a little (it was one of the kind that is hinged at the top and opens by swinging up and out from the bottom).

The fly had plenty of room to escape now, but he continued to fling himself frantically from one extreme to the other—always within the confines of the window frame.

One could understand this. After all, he had been at it for a long time and, although it wasn't getting the exact results desired, he had begun to feel at home with it and, well . . . safe; looking out there where he told

48

himself he wanted to be, and battering away, and looking, and battering, and . . . one could understand.

So I opened the window a lot more with the hope that this new position would bring new perspective—that he would grasp the situation and embrace his freedom.

He didn't. He was too busy trying to get out! It would seem that he had lived with the difficulty so long that the problem no longer involved such abstract concepts as 'freedom', or 'containment.' The problem was this window in front of him! He must get *through that window*! The window was still in front of him. Nothing had changed. The fact that the whole thing was now outside in the air had nothing to do with it!

So, with a little effort and a lot of sarcasm, I opened the window *all* the way. I opened it until it stood out at right angles to the side of the building. Now he would have to change his *direction* in order to remain contained! He would have to lie on his back defying the laws of gravity and batter himself vertically to maintain contact with the window!

He did! Something snapped! I remember flailing away at him like someone possessed, and his resisting all movement away from the window. It was a desperate battle, in doubt until the very end, when a last ditch effort made brief but firm contact and I flung him to fulfillment!

FIRST REFLECTION:
"THROUGH TRUST I ENTER IN"

It was by means of the parable of The Fly that Jesus invited me, many years ago, to stop battering myself to death trying to come out into freedom through my own efforts. He knew that I was in bondage to many things—primarily to fear—and he was asking me to accept him as the one who was doing everything necessary to give me more life and freedom than I could hope for or imagine. And I heard a promise: he would finish this work that he had begun in me. I could resist, of course. I could prolong the confusion and multiply the collisions. But I felt a magnificent assurance that his love would be victorious in me.

This was a profound challenge, shared with a gentle, infectious smile: a challenge to allow him to be for me what I could not be for myself. But it was also a loving challenge to join together with him in this wonderful work of coming into fuller life. He would not—could not—have victory *in* me *without* me. I was not to be the object of some divine improvement project, but an active participant in a great adventure. This was to be a collaboration. All this freeing work was to be done in the context of a relationship based on trust. Me, trusting God. The trust would bring me into the place where his love and power could set me free from my fear. I knew that to start, all I had to do was stop struggling, unclench my fists, and open my eyes; if I were to relax for even a minute I would fall right down into the strong, delivering hand of my Heavenly Father.

The key to everything was (and is) trust. To understand what this trust entails we might draw an analogy: it is as though the window where the battle with the fly was going on was a ticket window. At this window I needed to get a ticket that would allow me to enter in to the world outside. The ticket that would allow me to get in is called "faith." Out there, was the place called "grace". The land of grace.

The promise was that in this place of 'grace' there would be love and healing, joy and intimacy, acceptance and wisdom and mercy—all the power of the living God to give me a whole new life and to grow me up into his secure, mature child! With entry into this new land, all the gifts my Heavenly Father wanted to give me would be mine for the receiving and the living.

But what, exactly is this ticket called 'faith'? First it is my belief that all the above is true! This means that I believe the Truth which the Holy Spirit brings to me as a gift: there is one God who loves me, in Jesus Christ, perfectly and for my own sake; who knows, and desires, what is best for me; who has the will and the power to bring me full, free, eternal life; who has done all that is necessary so that that life can be mine—now and after my death.

Paul speaks of this aspect of faith in this well known passage: ". . . if you confess with your mouth, 'Jesus is Lord', and believe in your heart that God raised him from the dead, you will be saved [Romans10:9]. I want to say, "Yes Paul! That's the ticket"! But Paul knows that this "ticket"—this faith—is not what saves us. Paul often says that we are "saved by faith," but this is shorthand and serves another point. He is clear that it is not what we bring to the table (faith) that saves us; it is what God brings to the table (grace) that saves us [Romans 3:24]. Paul summarizes all his teaching about the relationship between our faith, God's grace, and our salvation in his letter to the Ephesians when he says, "It is by *grace* you are saved, *through faith*" [Ephesians. 2:8].

The ticket is not the main thing: the importance of having a ticket is not the possession of the ticket—it is that the ticket gains admittance for the holder into a particular place. The 'land of Grace' is the salvation site! Faith is what brings me into the place of God's saving grace.

But if that is true then faith is more than a ticket I 'hold in my hand.' It is more than what I *say* I believe, no matter how deeply and sincerely I may profess it. What I *really* 'believe' will be reflected in what I *do*. The faith that Paul refers to is the one that brings us into the place of grace.

Without that faith I would be like a person who, having just purchased a ticket, stands there with it in his hand saying, "Wow, I've got a ticket to 'Graceland'! I'm amazed! Jesus is Lord! I believe God his Father raised him from the dead!" And he goes from person to person rejoicing about how he's got this ticket of faith! Finally someone stops him.

"Say, buddy, I'm about to go on through to Graceland, want to come along?"

"What are you talking about? I'm *in* Graceland! Look, here it is."

"No, no. Who told you that? What you've got there is the *ticket* to Graceland. You have to take that ticket and move on through into the actual place."

"Well . . . I don't know. Somebody gave this to me. It was absolutely free—didn't cost me a thing! In fact they said that if it cost me anything it wasn't the real ticket. And they said not to believe anyone who said I would have to do anything *with* it. This ticket is the only thing I need. I love this ticket. This ticket is beautiful. Just holding it I feel better already!"

"Well, if you think the *ticket* is great, wait until you come into *grace*! Wow! That's the place where things *really* start happening! But you have to use the ticket. And it's going to cost you absolutely everything, just like Jesus said it would! You can't bring anything else with you through that door."

"I don't know about that. It looks scary over there. 'Faith alone!', that's what I always say! I think this ticket is enough. I know I believe the right thing because I know I've said the right thing. I like it here. I'll just stay here with the ticket. Thanks anyway."

The 'ticket' of faith means more than the thing I hold in my hand; more than what I say I believe; more than what I have confessed with my mouth. Faith must bring me out from where I am to the place where new life is found. The aspect of faith that brings me into grace is the very thing that I as a sinful, broken man find the most difficult: trust! And trust can only spring from what I truly believe in my heart!

In order to come into the place of grace I must actually put my confidence in God. I must rely on him. I must trust in his love and mercy and power. Actively! This is not the same thing as *saying* "I trust you." It is the actual trusting itself. This is what lies behind Paul's words about confessing and believing! [Romans 10:11].

Could it be that we have not accepted Jesus as 'Lord' simply because we have confessed the truth that *he is Lord*? Could it be that we have not effectively accepted Jesus as our Savior simply because we have said "Jesus, I accept you as my Savior"? Yes, it not only could be—it is. Jesus made this very clear. One of the most heart-breaking statements in all of scripture demonstrates Jesus' awareness that many would call him 'Lord' but not accept him: "Why do you call me 'Lord, Lord' and do not do what I say?" [Luke 6:46]. Could there be any clearer teaching? He is not our 'Lord' because we call him "Lord"! Jesus is our Lord if we actually yield lordship of our life to him; if we obey him by trusting him. And this is not accomplished as soon as we say "Jesus, I accept you as Lord, and I yield my whole life to you." These words are not magic and they do not cast a spell over God that blinds him to the truth of our hearts.

We are not saved by saying the right thing or even by believing the right thing. We are saved by the recreative power of the living God: by his grace. Many are ecstatically willing to give Jesus their "whole life" yet never give him any particular part of it. They believe in "his victory" but are not willing, in practice, to let him win that victory in them. And that victory is what we need. Time and time again! In every place within us.

Accepting Jesus means allowing him in so that he can win his victory in the "kingdom of us." Each of us is like an occupied, corrupt city. He becomes our Lord neighbourhood by neighbourhood, street by street, block by block. The life giving work of Jesus as Savior and Lord is done though costly house to house, room-by-room, hand-to-hand combat. We invite him into every pocket of resistance, into every pagan shrine and every garbage dump; into every dark room where a little one weeps and vows, where the one who was shamed burns with rage, and the abandoned one huddles, cold and alone.

So, of course we are not saved by believing the right thing *about* the Savior. Having truly believed, we are saved by *the saving work of the Savior,* but only because we have trusted him enough to allow him to come in and do his work in us. Am I saved by believing in the effectiveness of a surgical procedure and the competence of the physician? No. That informed, inspired trust must get me to the hospital. *True* faith gets us to the hospital.

Again and again Jesus teaches that what we *do* indicates both *what* and *in whom* we *really* believe! Our fervent protestations of faith do not blind Jesus to the truth of what we *do*! He tells a parable of two brothers ordered to go work in the field. One says "yes" but does not go. The other says "no" but ends up working [Matthew 21:28-31]. It is the one who *does* his father's will who is commended. There is no more convicting parable in all of Jesus' teaching. Do we actually suppose that "saved by grace, through faith" means that Jesus died for us so that we can have a nice warm feeling, say all the right things about what we believe, call him "Lord," and then go our own way? That is a legal arrangement. We wish it were that way. It is the legalistic "salvation" of the Pharisee. It is that desperate attempt to find a salvation which will allow us to remain in control of our lives—which will bypass the need to trust—which will leave our rebellious hearts untouched and unrepentant.

Jesus concludes the "sermon on the mount" by stating that life built on the rock of the kingdom can only be ours if we actually get on the rock!

It is not enough to listen to and "believe" all the teaching *about* the rock while remaining on the sand! [Matthew 7:24-27]. Jesus said, in effect, that there would be many fervent cries of "Lord, Lord" spoken from the sand: "Not everyone who says unto me, 'Lord, Lord' will enter the Kingdom of heaven, but the one who does the will of my Father who is in heaven" [Matthew 7:21]. What is the Father's will? It is that we would do his will, chiefly by entering into a relationship with him of complete dependence, based upon child-like trust [Matt. 18:1-4].

How would this look? What might we actually do that would be active trusting of Jesus? Perhaps a good fundamental way to start would be to yield a specific thing to him that is in our heart. This is how we "accept" him as our Savior: we invite him to save us from something real. Something personal. For instance, because he said he came to set the captives free, I might ask him to set me free from something that holds me in bondage. Maybe it is the deep well of fear and sadness, rooted in the death of my father when I was a child, that overflows into my life and threatens to drown me again and again. The dike of protection I have constructed around those bitter waters has become the wall of a prison, too strong for me to break down. I might come to him in prayer (it probably wouldn't be quite this simple, but it would be *like* this—it would *be* this, *in effect*):

"Lord, I'm afraid."

"I know."

"I've always been afraid."

"I know. I don't want you to live with that fear any more. Do you trust my love?"

"Yes. I think I do. I'm willing to let you have this. But I'm afraid. Help me, Jesus."

"I will. What do you see?"

"I see a young boy. His father has died. He is alone and cannot find his daddy. He is afraid. They are saying, 'He died', but what does it mean? I know this is me. I remember."

"Yes."

"Where were you, Jesus?"

"I was there."

"I want to see you there. Be there with me!"

These are obedient words of active trust. This trust brings me into the grace of Jesus' healing, transforming ministry. He honors my desire to meet with him in that place where my sinfulness and brokenness is rooted. He may meet with and minister to me in a solitary time of prayer. More often Jesus ministers in this way with the help of other persons who walk as children of the Father, and, having been given gifts by the Holy Spirit, are able to facilitate his work in others. The content of that healing ministry is both simple and powerfully effective beyond anything possible through merely human intervention.

When Jesus comes there in that memory and reveals himself to that frightened and confused little boy who has been running much of my life, I will certainly experience him with me in the present, as I expect, but I may also experience a mysterious dimension to this ministry: I may also experience Jesus as the "Lord of time", who ministers "then"! What "has been" is never the same again when I have met him there in "what was." Just as I do not know the truth of today unless I know Jesus here and now, so I do not know the truth of yesterday until I know Jesus there and then. My memory is not "The Truth", though it is my reality. Jesus is the Truth.

What I had that I call my reality consisted of lies, emptiness, abandonment, isolation, fear, and confusion. Now, through trust, I come out from *my "reality"* into *his truth*. Trust has entered into grace, and grace is flowing like a river, clean and sweet. Rather than a new strategy for coping, this is deep and profound cleansing and healing. The pain and fear are taken into the heart of Jesus. Jesus brings truth where lies had taken root. He brings a faithful embrace where there was emptiness and abandonment.

The actual *time* of traumatic wounding is *itself* transformed. The very memory is healed! It was a time when, through loss, fear became known. Now it has become a time when, through the same experience of that same loss, the compassion, strength and love of Jesus is experienced and known as he meets with me there and then. In the sea-change effected by the stream of his living water flowing through me, I am swept out from abandonment into loving presence. From bewilderment and confusion into the calm clarity of consoling embrace. From curse into blessing. From death into life.

Believing in him, accepting him, inviting him—all this is part of it. Active trusting completes the faith that brings me into the place of his great power—the place of grace, mercy, and love. Through trusting I become available to the God whose power creates me new as his beloved child.

No matter what I say I believe, no matter what I have spoken with my lips, unless I actively trust God to be God for me, I continue the life that is not life at all. It is not hard to distinguish between the fruit of that counterfeit life and the fruit of the life of trust (saving faith). Since trust brings me into the place of graceful transformation, the difference can be seen in the person I am becoming. As a person transformed by the grace of God, I begin to do the wonderful, costly things that flow "naturally" from a heart where my Savior has been invited and received in all his truth and with all his healing, creative power.

What I *do* flows from who I *am*! Therefore, the things I do will indicate whether or not (or to what extent) I have truly entered into the place of grace. I "have the ticket," but have I used it? You will know by the fruit of my life. (James speaks of this very clearly [James 2:14-24], but if we only took our blinkers off we would see that Paul does too, as in Romans 8:3-5 and 12-17.). Without trust, no matter what I say I believe, I will continue, like the fly, to fling myself "from one extreme to the other, all within the confines of the window frame!"

"I see the land of grace out there." [Whap!]

"I want to go there." [Smack!]

"I believe in you, Jesus!" [Whap! Whap!]

"I . . . [smack!] . . . I trust you." [Whap! Whap!]

"It's me and you, Jesus!" [Smack!]

The truth about the One we can trust is this: God (Father, Son, and Holy Spirit] has done, and is doing, everything necessary so that his love and his life can be victorious in us. The window is fully open. If we were to stop struggling, unclench our fists, and open our eyes; if we were to relax for even a minute; *if we were to put our trust in him*, we would fall right down into the strong, loving hands of the Living God.

First Reflection In A Nutshell
"Through Trust I Enter In"

We have explored the means by which we come into the place where God's power can effectively impact our lives and set us free. Jesus meets us in that place where we struggle to find freedom through our own unaided efforts. Trust is the 'ticket' that brings us into the place of grace—the place where the power of God meets us very personally and accomplishes in us what we cannot accomplish apart from him.

Questions for reflection or discussion

1. Are you battering yourself to death trying to come out into freedom through your own efforts? Share with Jesus the truth about what you see as you reflect on your life "within the confines of the window frame." Invite Jesus to show you those places in your life where you trust him least and where you trust him most.
2. Do you believe it is possible that you have entered the 'land of grace' in some areas of your life but that in other areas you continue to struggle at the window? Do you know that the window where you are "battering yourself vertically" has been fully opened? What does that mean to you?
3. Has anyone ever told you that they trusted you, but their behavior indicated that they did not? Have you experienced in your own life the very real difference between saying to God "I trust you" and the actual trusting itself?
4. "What I really 'believe' will be [seen] in what I [actually] do." Reflect on this statement in terms of those areas in your life where you trust God least: what does your actual behavior tell you about what you really believe?
5. "Now, through trust, I come out from my 'reality' into his truth." Reflect on the difference between the "reality" we live with and the "truth" Jesus knows (and is), in the light of this description: ". . . I am swept out from abandonment into loving presence. From bewilderment and confusion into the calm clarity of consoling embrace."

MEDITATION ON PSALM 9
"I will give thanks to you, O Lord, with my whole heart."

There is one thing I know, Lord. I'm going to praise you. I'm going to be glad in you—rejoice in you. Out of my heart is coming (is going to come) a song about what you do; a song about who you are: that much I know. Many things I do not know. I'm troubled by what seems to be: rebellion and wickedness having their way. Then I see how evil puts itself to death—there I catch a glimpse of your perfect justice. I see. You are sovereign. Then I don't see, Lord. Not really. The needy seem to be forgotten; the hope of the persecuted seems to have died. Men go on and on believing they are more than men. And they seem to have their way. And I suffer. And I cause suffering. Do you see, Lord?

One thing I do know: I can flee to you. Maybe there is another thing I know: what seems to be is not all of what is. I do know that I am blind to many things but that you see all that is. One more thing I know: those who flee to you—who seek you with their whole heart—will find you. I know that is true and so I know that I will praise you and I know that though men seem to reign for a time, you reign before time and for all time and beyond all time; I know that we men and women seem to be, but you, Lord, are. I do not want to *seem*, I want to *be*. I will praise you. I will flee to you. In you, Lord, *I am*!

SCRIPTURAL SCENE:
"GOD WILL PROVIDE THE LAMB"

Genesis 22:1-14a

Sometime later God tested Abraham. He said to him, "Abraham!" "Here I am," he replied.

Then God said, "Take your son, your only son, Isaac, whom you love, and go to the region of Moriah. Sacrifice him there as a burnt offering on one of the mountains I will tell you about."

Early the next morning Abraham got up and saddled his donkey. He took with him two of his servants and his son Isaac. When he had cut enough wood for the burnt offering, he set out for the place God had told him about. On the third day Abraham looked up and saw the place in the distance. He said to his servants, "Stay here with the donkey while I and the boy go over there. We will worship and then we will come back to you."

Abraham took the wood for the burnt offering and placed it on his son Isaac, and he himself carried the fire and the knife. As the two of them went on together, Isaac spoke up and said to his father Abraham, "Father?"

"Yes, my son?" Abraham replied.

"The fire and wood are here," Isaac said, "but where is the lamb for the burnt offering?"

Abraham answered, "God himself will provide the lamb for the burnt offering, my son." And the two of them went on together.

When they reached the place God had told him about, Abraham built an altar there and arranged the wood on it. He bound his son Isaac and laid him on the altar, on top of the wood. Then he reached out his hand and took the knife to slay his son. But the angel of the LORD called out to him from heaven, "Abraham! Abraham!"

"Here I am," he replied.

"Do not lay a hand on the boy," he said. "Do not do anything to him. Now I know that you fear God, because you have not withheld from me your son, your only son." Abraham looked up and there in a thicket he saw a ram caught by its horns. He went over and took the ram and sacrificed it as a burnt offering instead of his son. So Abraham called that place The LORD Will Provide.

SECOND REFLECTION:
"THE TRUST OF ABRAHAM"

Which of us who are fathers would not give our life for our son or daughter? And which mothers would not give their life for their daughter or their son? The love that we feel for our children is beyond what words can express. Most of us cannot imagine anything worse than the loss of a child. Few of us can imagine surviving such a loss as a whole person with a sound mind and a healthy spirit. I am convinced that no one does so without a tremendous outpouring of the grace of God.

Would Abraham have felt any different about his son? If God had asked, would he have hesitated to give his own life for that of Isaac? I do not think so.

But this was a far more difficult thing than that. Abraham was not asked to give his life for Isaac. He was told to sacrifice his son's life, and for no other apparent reason than God's unelaborated command.

God begins by reminding Abraham of his great love for Isaac: this Isaac who was born to Sarah after all hope of her ever giving birth was gone. This son was God's living, breathing miracle. Earlier, laughter had bubbled from them both at the absurdity of a too-old, barren woman giving birth. Later they laughed with joy and wonder. Now Abraham is being told not only to give up his beloved Isaac, but to take his son's life with his own hands.

Why did God demand this of Abraham? Scripture tells us that God was testing him. The angel seems to indicate at first that the issue is the fear of God: "Now I know that you fear God . . . ." However, the point may not be the 'fear'. The point seems to be that he did what God told him to do. This is made explicit later, in verse 18: ". . . and through your offspring all nations on earth will be blessed, *because you have obeyed me.*" [The emphasis is mine.]

However, the question remains: *why put Abraham to the test at all?* True, he had not always been perfectly obedient. After God had made it clear, twice, that it was Sarah who would bear him the child of the promise [Genesis 17:15f, 18:10], our "father in faith", in order to secure his own safety, passed Sarah off as his sister so that she ended up in the hands of the ruler Abimelech, and, for all he knew, lost to him and to her crucial role in the fulfillment of God's expressed purposes [Genesis. 20]!

This, you may be sure, was not "credited to him as righteousness"! It is true—there was 'room for growth' as far as Abraham went, concerning obedience.

But why try his obedience *now*? The covenant was in place, the son was conceived and born and growing, if not grown. To put it crudely—didn't God have something better to do? Hadn't Abraham served his purpose? What more was there for him to do that would require some new dimension of obedience? The *big* events were over. Abraham had little left to do but settle the conflict involving Ishmael, bury Sarah, come up with a plan to get a wife for Isaac, and father the Asshurites, the Letushites, and the Leummites. Granted that these things have some importance, and must have put at least his endurance to the test, none required an *extraordinary* amount of obedience to carry out.

I believe that God's focus was somewhere else. The answer lies in something other than Abraham's utility. Abraham was not just someone that God 'used' as a major player in a magnificent unfolding drama of salvation. *God loved Abraham.* He would continue to call Abraham into a deeper place with him, no matter his "usefulness". The God of Abraham wanted more of *Abraham*. And he wanted to reveal his heart to the 'father of nations' and, I believe, to the 'nations' that would follow: to us.

Where was the "growing edge" in Abraham—what was it, exactly, that God was calling forth in him? We could simply say "obedience". We have already seen that, in the end, this is what God commended him for. But obedience does not stand alone. It rests on something else. We obey for a reason. *Why* did Abraham obey? In order to 'pass' this test, what did Abraham need in abundance? Was it "fear"? This can certainly be a motive for obedience. According to the message delivered by the angel, it seems that fear was part of what God was producing in Abraham. A fear that leads to obedience. Of course, we are not talking about "fear" as in "I'm afraid of the dark," or "I'm afraid of the big bad man over there." Rather a "fear" that is awed reverence for the goodness, majesty, faithfulness, power, glory, and sovereignty of God.

But there must be more. There is not a lot to go on in the story that would point to "fear", by any definition, as the *primary* motive in the heart of Abraham. What one observes is a solid calmness, almost a matter-of-factness, with which he goes about preparing to leave. Later, he speaks to his servants and to Isaac with a quiet confidence and strength—almost a tenderness (". . . we will come back to you . . . yes, my son . . . God will provide . . ."). What did it take for Abraham to be this way and do this thing? Awe was there, surely. But I agree with Paul (always a wise choice): it was faith—specifically *trust*—that lay at the heart of God's call to Abraham. Trust was the indispensable, human response which God sought and commended—the only motive in the human heart that could lead to an acceptable ('righteous') relationship with him [Romans 4:5]. Wisdom began in Abraham as awe-filled reverence for the holiness and sovereignty of the Lord, but wisdom found its mature fulfillment in trust.

The place of trust was the place of testing in the heart of Abraham. In order to do what God had commanded him to do, Abraham would have to find within himself the capacity for a whole new level of trust. But trust had always been the issue.

His journey with God had begun in trust when God called him to leave his homeland and go to a strange new country. In this new place, Abraham had been sustained by God's promise to him. This land of Canaan, now occupied by others, was to be given to his descendents, who would become a great nation, as numerous as the stars. God would pour out his blessing on them, and, through them, he would bless all nations.

This was the crux of the testing of Abraham: the only way, according to the word of God, that the promise of God could be fulfilled was through Abraham's son, Isaac. Without the future generations that would come from Isaac, the promise was empty. And now the very God who had made the promise was telling Abraham to give up the only means of its fulfillment! [Hebrews 11:17ff]

Abraham was called to choose. What, exactly, was he going to put his trust *in*? The promise, and his understanding of how the promise was to be fulfilled? *Or was he going to trust the God who made the promise?* Everything circumstantial mocked and drove against trust. *This* trust would have to be based on God's faithfulness alone.

Let us imagine the interior dialogue Abraham held with himself at the time of testing:

Abraham: "You really wanted the land and the progeny, the nation and the blessing that God promised earlier. It made a kind of sense to the hopeful place in you. And in Sarah. You both laughed, but you yearned for a son. You didn't see how it would happen, but everything in you wanted to trust God. So you did."

Himself:	"Yes."
Abraham:	"And the Sovereign Lord honored that. It was overwhelming."
Himself:	"Yes."
Abraham:	"But that trust didn't cost you much, did it?"
Himself:	"That's not entirely . . . ."
Abraham:	"Did it?"
Himself:	"Well . . . I had to go on having relations with that old woman, my wife!" *[He cannot completely hide his smile.]*
Abraham:	"That was her trial, not yours, Abraham!"
Himself:	"Was that you, Lord?"
	[Silence . . . But the Sovereign Lord does not completely hide his smile.]
Abraham:	"This thing the Lord has told you to do . . . this is different. There is nothing about this that you desire. You love Isaac. There is no reason in this. No wisdom. It is the destruction of all your hope. This will cost you everything!"
Himself:	"Yes." *[He weeps.]*
The Sovereign Lord:	"Will you trust me, Abraham?"
Abraham Himself:	*[He falls on his face.]* "Yes! Yes Lord. Yes!"

With this "yes" Abraham made his choice: he chose to surrender to God the things that he loved the most, including things that, as a father, he loved more than he loved his own life. He was willing to give up his son and his hope, in one act of uncommon and costly obedience, rooted in radical trust. This new dimension of trust brought Abraham into the place of God's grace. This grace came to him as an assurance of provision and as a profound revelation of the heart of God.

Grace came first as Abraham *received* the assurance of God's provision for him. He named the place where he was to have sacrificed his son, "The Lord will provide." Surely this was deeply felt. His trust had proved costly indeed! The further he went the more it must have cost him. What price did he pay as he said, "God himself will provide the lamb for the burnt offering, my son." What price did he pay as he bound him to the altar? Abraham was a human person as we are. Perhaps just a little bit of his trust included the hope that God would intervene. Even if that was so, the last of that element in his trust would have trickled out like water as he wound those cords around his precious son.

And what did it cost him to take hold of the knife?

Right at this point of crisis, the result of Abraham's act of trust, grace is opened to him in a second way: the heart of the Sovereign Lord is revealed. Through trust, Abraham came to know the heart of the God of Abraham. He learned that the God who is awesome does not require the sacrifice of children. God did not accept the sacrifice of Abraham's son. God himself provided for the sacrifice.

"Abraham, Abraham . . ."! In that moment, through the voice of an angel calling him by name, the loving provision of God was deeply impressed upon Abraham's heart. Yes, and upon the hearts of all the offspring of his trust down through the ages. Carried in the hearts of his people, this promise from the heart of God—this revelation of his provision and his saving plan—is now blessed and endlessly multiplied, finding fulfillment in the hearts of those who trust and receive the gift of life offered by another beloved Son, who became a Lamb for us.

Second Reflection In A Nutshell
"The Trust of Abraham"

In this reflection we note that God drew Abraham into deeper and deeper dimensions of trust. This growing trust brought him into the place of grace where the Sovereign Lord reveals the nature of his heart and the depth of his loving, life-giving provision to Abraham and to all who trust as he did.

Questions for reflection or discussion

1. Imagine yourself on a mountain hike. You come upon a man who, having bound his son to an altar, is about to kill him with a knife. You scream and tell him to stop. The man insists that God has told him to do this. What do you say to him?

2. Do you "fear God"? What do you understand that to mean? Has your understanding changed over time?

3. "Abraham was not just someone that God 'used' as a major player in a magnificent unfolding drama of salvation." Do you believe that your main value to God consists in your usefulness to him? Does God "use" people? Would that be the same or different from the way we might "use" a shovel?

4. How big is the issue of obedience to God in your life? Look at some area of your life where you think you are at least somewhat obedient. Why are you obedient—what does your obedience 'rest on'?

5. "Trust was the indispensable, human response which God sought and commended—the only motive in the human heart that could lead to an acceptable ("righteous") relationship with him [Romans 4:5]." What do you think it is about trust that makes it 'indispensable' in our relationship with God?

6. "Abraham made his choice: he chose to surrender to God the things that he loved the most . . . ." Are you willing to surrender to God the things—and the people—that you love the most? What does this mean to you? What would keep you from doing it? What/who do you love more than you love God?

MEDITATION ON PSALM 13
"But I put my trust in your mercy"

From a life in music . . . .

Almost 15 years ago these words came to me (this particular psalm). This was before the large steps of believing that followed; before I opened the door for Jesus so widely that if I were to push him out and shut that door again, it would require an unthinkably violent turning—a reach so far into the darkness that it would rip and tear every connective tissue within me. (If that door where you entered was closed and you outside a second time, Jesus, I know I would be more completely alone, more heartbroken, and in deeper death than was possible before the knock was first heard or the door first opened.)

The first four verses, coming at that time, were my personal heart's cry. Those words became music easily, powerfully; so smoothly translated that nothing was lost in the journeys, psalm to song—heart to head to heart. I was the psalm becoming song until the shock of the last two verses: "But I put my trust in your mercy; my heart is joyful because of your saving help . . . I will sing . . . I will praise . . . !" Here was a musical problem of the first order! I was stumped. I was offended. "How did we get *here*," I cried! "We've come from 'How long, O Lord, will you forget me forever . . . . ', to all this trusting, and joy, and praise for saving help and rich blessing, with *no transition whatsoever*? We just leap from one to the other? Is this credible? Does this have integrity: a crude cup of swamp despair one minute, a champagne toast the next?!" How could this be made to work *musically*? I could not see an honest way through.

Then the deeper issue spoke in me: "How can this work *spiritually*?" I realized I could not truthfully, creatively, or expressively bring these last verses into song because the truth they creatively expressed was not embraced and fully living in me. I needed to choose to yield in a new way: to learn deeper trust. The turning point in the psalm and the song was now a turning-point in me. If this song was to be completed, I would have to be completed: this new song would need to find its finish in a new person.

I set the song aside for several months. When I took it up again it was with hands that had reached out to open the door fully. The music flowed from a freer, lighter heart. The Lord heard my cry: "Give light to my eyes, lest I sleep in death." Now, by His light my eyes could see the way from confusion and complaint to trust. The transition was accomplished musically and spiritually: we get from here to there by the light of His rising in us.

"Wake up, O sleeper,
Rise from the dead,
And Christ will shine on you!"

[Ephesians 5:14]

SCRIPTURAL SCENE:
"HE CANNOT SAVE HIMSELF"

Luke 23:33-46

When they came to the place called the Skull, there they crucified him, along with the criminals—one on his right, the other on his left. Jesus said, "Father, forgive them, for they do not know what they are doing." And they divided up his clothes by casting lots.

The people stood watching, and the rulers even sneered at him. They said, "He saved others; let him save himself if he is the Christ of God, the Chosen One."

The soldiers also came up and mocked him. They offered him wine vinegar and said, "If you are the king of the Jews, save yourself."

There was a written notice above him, which read: THIS IS THE KING OF THE JEWS.

One of the criminals who hung there hurled insults at him: "Aren't you the Christ? Save yourself and us!"

But the other criminal rebuked him. "Don't you fear God," he said, "since you are under the same sentence? We are punished justly, for we are getting what our deeds deserve. But this man has done nothing wrong."

Then he said, "Jesus, remember me when you come into your kingdom."

Jesus answered him, "I tell you the truth, today you will be with me in paradise."

It was now about the sixth hour, and darkness came over the whole land until the ninth hour, for the sun stopped shining. And the curtain of the temple was torn in two. Jesus called out with a loud voice, "Father, into your hands I commit my spirit." When he had said this, he breathed his last.

THIRD REFLECTION:
"THE TRUST OF JESUS"

For Jesus, the horrible day of his betrayal and suffering is ending. He has been mocked and slapped and spat on and struck with fists. He has been whipped and jeered at and stripped and nailed naked to a cross. Not satisfied, his torturers have hurled bitter insults like weapons, as though they'd kill him a second time if they could—with words. He is mocked, first by the rulers who stand beneath him, then by one of the criminals who hangs beside him: "He saved others; let him save himself if he is the Christ of God."

The criminal has a vested interest in whatever "saving" Jesus might be able to do: "Aren't you the Christ? Save yourself and us!" This man is not only in physical agony, but his words betray bitterness. At the root of his bitterness may be the conviction that he is suffering unjustly. And maybe he is right, at least in part. We do sometimes suffer unjustly in this life.

Some of our suffering is not the result of any sinful choice we have made. You may remember that Jesus acknowledged this once when his disciples asked him about a certain man who had been born blind. They wanted to know if he was blind because he had sinned, or because his parents had sinned. Jesus said, "neither this man nor his parents sinned" [John 9:1-3].

But most of the time that is not the case—or certainly it is not that cut and dried. We may be innocent, but on the other hand, maybe we are not *so* innocent. Others have done things to us, but we have played our part too. And then some.

The second criminal calls the other man and himself to an honest accounting. "We have been condemned justly, for we are getting what we deserve for our deeds, but this man has done nothing wrong."

For the criminal, that was the moment of faith. But in order for him to come to faith, he had to begin with the truth. He did this when he acknowledged that Jesus was suffering for a different reason than he was. In order to acknowledge this truth, he had to turn toward Jesus, and away from resentment and bitterness.

The truth seen in that turning was that there was more than one kind of suffering going on there at Golgotha. He confessed that his suffering was the result of his own sinful choosing.

When he acknowledged the truth about his own suffering and turned to Jesus, he began, in a sense, to share in Christ's suffering. This was the suffering of one who was not getting what he 'deserved.' The criminal said that this Jesus was not dying because he had done something he should not have done. He understood at least half the truth. We know the whole truth: it was far more than just a case of his being innocent of the particular acts of disobedience of which he was accused—Jesus' suffering issued from true and perfect obedience rooted in his love of the Father and his desire to do the Father's will. But, with incomplete understanding, this man, acting on the little he did know, turned to Jesus in faith.

Faith must have come to this dying man, as it comes to us all, as a gift, but we might wonder what things served as vehicles for its coming. Perhaps Jesus' words of forgiveness ("Father forgive them . . . .") spoken from the cross came to him in power. It may be that he was the first man in the world to take them to heart!

We could suppose that he read the sign over Jesus' cross which proclaimed him "king of the Jews." Pilate had intended this as a derisive slap in the face of Jesus and all the conquered, humbled Hebrew people. But Pilate had unwittingly proclaimed the truth and, perhaps, the ironic truth of it rose like a supernatural dawn in the thief's heart.

He may have drawn close to the Savior through his trusting choice to believe that this thing that was happening—this terrible thing—this death—was not to be the *last* thing. There, closer to him than even the short physical distance that separated them, the criminal wanted whatever it was that this 'King' could give him: "Jesus, remember me when you come into your Kingdom."

But by whatever subtle yet loving means God caused faith to spring up in his heart, we *know* faith motivated his request because of the words that Jesus spoke in response. The criminal's suffering did not end in that moment. His circumstance remained the same, but in the midst of his suffering, Jesus spoke words of living hope—words that could only come as a response to faith: "Truly, I tell you, today you will be with me in paradise."

Can you imagine what those words must have meant to the criminal? Under the law he was condemned, and he hung there in the agony of that truth. But with Jesus there was no condemnation. Can there be any doubt that right there and then that suffering man began to be lifted out of his world of hopelessness and despair? Can there be any doubt that right there and then he began to be with Jesus in paradise?

I believe Jesus makes the same promise to us. When we take a minute off from protesting our innocence and turn to him, we find that Jesus is right there with us—full of truth and love. He offers us forgiveness. When we are willing to be with Jesus in his suffering, we find that he offers us the possibility of being with him in paradise. Right there in the midst of our suffering, he draws us very close; and that closeness with Jesus is paradise.

We do not have the choice to suffer or not to suffer. Suffering will come. The choice is between suffering as a result of a self-inflicted wound, or suffering with Jesus. If we are determined to go on suffering from our sinfulness then we can manage that without Jesus. But if, from a desire to share intimate companionship with Jesus, we want to enter into his sufferings, then we are going to have to turn to him, because we cannot do it without him. The only way we can suffer with Christ is to live his life: the life of obedient love. The life of faith. The life of trust.

The good news is that when we turn to Jesus on the cross, we find that he is there in power, making it possible for us to confess the truth about our lives. When, like the criminal, we turn to Jesus, we see that he has become wounded so that we can be healed. When we turn to Jesus, he turns to us and speaks words of forgiveness and hope. When we turn to him in faith, he meets us in faith and we know beyond knowing that we need this faith that Jesus has. As we mature, we come to understand that our faith *in* Jesus is a great gift meant to lead us to receive an even greater gift: the faith *of* Jesus, that we might truly believe *what he believes* and trust *as he trusts*.

It was the faith of Jesus that made the faith of the criminal possible. He turned to Jesus in trust, but that was only possible because Jesus was there. This is painfully obvious but it is the key. I repeat: the criminal could not have turned to Jesus in trust (and entered into paradise) if Jesus had not come to be there on the cross next to him. It took no faith for the criminals to be there, but Jesus was there because he loved and trusted his Father. Before the thief trusted, Jesus trusted. In fact he opened the way of trust (faith) by going that way first. He is the perfect 'pioneer' of that way [Hebrews 12:2].

Strangely enough, it is not the honest accounting or trust of the second thief, but rather the mockery of the rulers and the other criminal that leads us most directly into the depth of the trust of Jesus, as perfectly demonstrated through his death on the cross. "He saved others, let him save himself!" These words are a slap in the face of his powerlessness. The implication is that, of course, he cannot save himself. The witnesses of Matthew and Mark make this explicit: "He saved others . . . but he *can't* save himself!" [Matthew 27:42; Mark 15:31; emphasis mine].

They, of course, believe that in order to "save" himself, Jesus must get down from the cross. They think this kind of 'saving' will authenticate the claim that he is the Messiah. They do not know that if he saves himself in this way he invalidates the claim. They do not know that if he 'saves' himself this way, he is lost. Jesus does not need—nor is he looking—to be saved from the cross, but from death itself. He has not come to defeat pain or avoid death through the use of self-serving power, but rather to defeat death itself, for us, by entering it in powerless trust.

And so it was that those who mocked spoke the truth. Jesus could not save himself. How could his way have become our way if Jesus could have saved himself? We cannot save ourselves! Jesus could not open the way that would become our way by just *pretending* to go that way . . . he had to actually go! Jesus was no more able to resurrect himself than we are. The witness of scripture is consistent: Jesus Christ really died and was raised to new "embodied" life *by God the Father Almighty*. He didn't do it himself. Jesus made this clear [Matthew 17:23], and there was never any confusion about it in the witness of the Apostles from the first Pentecostal proclamation onward [Acts 2:24; Romans 10:9]. Jesus could not save himself. He could only trust that the Father would raise him up.

Now we can see that it was not just the Word of Truth and the Word of Love, but also the Word of Trust that was crucified on Golgotha. Saving Faith was put to death on the cross. Faith can be the way of life for us only because the faith of Jesus was raised up by the Father in the Risen Lord and is available to us now through our trust in him! "We are saved by grace, through faith!" That is the saving way opened for us by the Father's plan. But it is our way only because Jesus walked it first.

The trust that Jesus had in his Father brought him into the place of grace. But what, ultimately, was that place of 'grace' for Jesus? It was *Resurrection Life* with the Father, freely given in love! He had to be raised up into this new life *by* the Father. It was only by 'Grace' that he could return to his Father from whom he came. The Father's part was raising him up to new life: he was saved *by grace*. His part was doing the Father's will in trust: he was saved *through faith*.

When we look at Jesus' life of faithful trusting, we see that trust in God is inseparable from obedience to God. As "the Word made flesh," Jesus could not return to the Father without accomplishing the purpose for which he was sent [Isaiah 55:10-11]. For Jesus, "grace" could only come in the context of the fulfillment of his commission from the Father—only through perfectly faithful completion of the Father's will. Avoiding the cross by whatever means, including the intervention of angels, would mean the abandonment of the Father's plan. Coming down from the cross by whatever power would only spell the end to, and utter failure of, Jesus' ministry of reconciliation, because the only possible path to the Father *for us* was the one that went through death [John 12:27]. This was the path of faith opened to us by the perfect trust of Jesus which lead him to the cross. He pleaded with the Father to open another way if it were possible. But there was no other way. There was only the way of death and resurrection. There was only the way of trust expressed through obedience. The way of obedience expressed through trust!

The world could sneer and mock but Jesus knew himself and so he knew the truth that the cross was the only "safe" place in all the world for him; the only place where he could be who he was and glorify the Father; the only place where he could overcome the world; the only place from which he could enter again into the glory he had with the Father before the world began [John 17:1-5].

He was not on the cross because he had done something wrong. He was there because he had done something perfectly right and done it supremely well. His death was not a failure but a crowning success. His suffering death was not irrefutable evidence that his trust had been misplaced. Rather it was the ultimate expression of the extent of that trust. His resurrection was his vindication, and a demonstration, for all with eyes to see and ears to hear, of the glorious truth that the One in whom he trusted was trust*worthy*!

It is true that "the righteous will live by faith" [Romans 1:17]. But before we could have life by faith, Jesus had to sow the seed of that life. The seed of his life-by-faith was deeply sown into good soil through his death [John 12:24].

There were many mocking words delivered at the foot of the cross, but God was not mocked. What is sown must be reaped. And it was. And it is. Jesus is the *Great Sower*. He sowed his life for love's sake; he scattered his life in trust. Because he sowed himself for the whole sinful world, the seed of his Father's saving way can grow in the hearts of those who mourn *and* those who mock, if only they turn to him in trust.

But he is also the great and loving reaper: Jesus gathered to himself the harvest of our sinful human sowing. Because he gathered the fruit of our rebellion, we can reap what he has sown, gathering the fruit of his obedience.[consider Galatians 6:8].

Jesus lived life-by-faith and offered up that life in trust so that we could believe *what he believes* and trust *as he trusts*. Unless we do, we cannot live his life. Unless we have the faith *of* Christ we cannot walk as he walked [1 John 2:6]. In the soil of our trust in him, the seed of the trusting life of our Savior grows and multiplies until that day when he gathers in the full harvest of those who love him.

Third Reflection In A Nutshell
"The Trust of Jesus"

Here we see Jesus as the one who goes before us as the "pioneer of our faith." He trusts his Father as we must. His trust brings him into the place of grace, just as our saving faith must if we are to enter into his life. Because he has opened the way, our faith *in* Christ makes it possible for us to have the faith *of* Christ.

Questions for reflection and/or discussion

1. One of the two criminals "confessed that his suffering was the result of his own sinful choosing." Have you suffered in your life from self-inflicted wounds? Did you have that awareness at the time?

2. "Jesus' suffering issued from true and perfect obedience rooted in his love of the Father and his desire to do the Father's will." Have you experienced any suffering which you believe resulted from your (not necessarily "perfect") obedience to God's will? Did you experience "fellowship with him" in that suffering?

3. "As we mature, we come to understand that our faith in Jesus is a great gift meant to lead us to receive an even greater gift: the faith of Jesus!" Reflect on this statement in the light of Paul's description of his life of faith: "It is not I who lives but Christ who lives in me."

4. What kind of power did Jesus have that made it possible for him "to defeat death itself, for us, by entering it in powerless trust"?

5. Why do you suppose it is that "trust in God is inseparable from obedience to God"? It is true that trust in God is always an expression of obedience, but is the reverse also true: that obedience is always an expression of trust?

PRAYING THE SCRIPTURE, PART 3
"Because I live, you also will live."

Thank you, Jesus, for the life you are. And thank you for your promise and your truth expressed so simply and clearly, calling me back to you, in whom I begin and end—wooing me away from so many things that parade as life, but which have no life. Please Lord, be with me and rehearse the truth within me:

I thank you that I don't have life because I've been good today. I praise you that I don't have life because of my understanding of things spiritual. Thank you that I don't have life because I feel deeply, or because people praise me. Thank you that I don't have life because I am creative, or because I've suffered and endured. I praise you that I don't have life because I believe you died for me, or because I know you love me. All these things are good, Jesus. Some are very good. I rejoice in them. But I have life because you live.

The world tells me to "get a life." Well (praise you!) I got a life. I was given a life when you gave yourself to me. You are the only life I want. Come, Jesus, live in me more fully, even in this moment. I want you to come where I have resisted life. Come Lord, reveal the dark place in me. Come Jesus, light up the tomb in me. I want to come humbly and boldly out from that tomb—not resuscitated but resurrected; not emerging into *my* "life" again, but into *yours*.

Any other life but you is wearing out. You are, eternally, life-with-the-Father. And I don't have life because I know that truth about you. I have life because you have life. You live. Life is you. You and your Father spoke that truth in ages past: "I AM." I thank and praise you that because YOU ARE, *I am*.

I receive you into my heart and mind—into the place where I am with me. Because you live there, I will know the Way. Because you live, I will know the Truth. Because you live, I will know Life. Because you live, love, hope and trust will live in me.

I yield to your life, Jesus. I trust your life. I want only your life. Be life for me when I know fear. Strengthen me and show me the way to your life when I know anger, shame, jealousy, or judgment.

I yield to your life, Jesus. I trust your life. I want only your life: life that comes through death and resurrection; life that is taken, blessed, broken . . . given.

I love you. Thank you, Jesus.

C hapter Four

INTIMACY:
"A Place Where We Choose To Be"

The business of choosing becomes the point increasingly as we move with God into fuller life. We come to understand that our desire and power to choose God is rooted in God's having desired and chosen us. Though we cannot choose without his grace, we must, by his grace, choose!

SCENE: "YOU WANT TO BE WITH ME!"

[A man kneels to pray. He is obviously uncomfortable. He looks around, he adjusts his clothing, then tries closing his eyes. Ten seconds go slowly by before he opens them again. He looks up, then down, then straight ahead. He sighs. Then, eyes wide open, he launches.]

He: O God. I'm here, but I don't know how to be here. I want to pray, but I don't know how to pray.
[There is a long silence. He is aware of nothing other than his own distractions. Finally, a thought comes . . . moving gently . . . he feels something too . . . fleeting but sweet . . . can it be from God?]

He: Is that you, God? It's probably just me . . . my mind is racing . . . I'm all over the place! If I could just be . . . here. Here with nothing better to do—content to just be where I am. I remember what that's like. I remember the first day of vacation when my children were small. The car's in motion. If we get there, fine. If not, fine. There's a sense of weightlessness—the burden's lifted. Nothing to solve. No deadline to meet. No one pressing me to do any particular thing.

God: Let it be like that. Let me drive.

He: O God, I had an idea that this time—this prayer time—could be a free time like that vacation. You could drive! I want to be with you, God, not just me talking to myself. I want to pray. I want to hear you! *[Silence, and then softer.]* But there's no way today's a vacation. Everybody has a claim on me. Everybody has an expectation. There is no "me" separate from what I have to do.

God: And yet you're here. Just be here.

He: Every minute I spend here in prayer—or whatever this is—is one less minute I'll have to do all the things I *have* to do today, not to mention the things I would *like* to do . . . for me. There's never any time for me!

God: There is this time. Do you want this time for you?

He: Lord, I want this time for me! I'm here because they said it would be good for me—quiet time—time alone—time for prayer. And I want that. But whenever I'm quiet and alone and trying to just relax and be—trying to speak to you, listen to you—all these other

things keep rushing at me: worries, regrets . . . the truth is I don't like being alone . . . Especially with me . . . that's a joke.
[He smiles—he is not alone in the smile.]

God: I love being with you.
[And then, with perfect timing:]
But of course I *have* to . . . I'm God!
["He" laughs out loud . . . a brief explosion.]

God: I love to be with you.

He: *[Pause]* Lord, somehow I get the feeling that you actually *want* to be with me! You couldn't possibly want to be with me—I don't even want to be with me. That proves these thoughts are not from you. It's just me.
[After some time.] When I'm alone I can't stop thinking of things I've done that are horrible. I'm such a rotten person sometimes. The truth is, I disgust myself. I make myself sick. If you only knew some of the . . . .

God: I know.
[There is a long pause.]

He: Everything? I guess I knew that . . . I almost never think of it. But if you already know everything about me, and about everything else for that matter, why do I bother? Why pray? What do you need to know from me?
[Silence.]

God: I want to know you. I want to be with you. Just be with me.

He: I don't know how to be with you.

God: Be who you are.

He: I don't know who I am. Besides, I couldn't be with God . . . with . . . you . . . the way I *really* am, even if I did know who I am—I know that much. I don't want you to see me that way. I can't talk to *you* about . . . but of course you already . . . O this is all in my head anyway! I'm making you up!

God: Well! The truth is that I made you up! *[A pause.]* And I love what I have made.
[It is clear that "he" is stricken by this, and struggling.]
I am with you in your mind—that is true. I am also with you in your heart. I'm always with you. I want to share the love that is in my heart with you. I want to tell you who you are to me. Share

81

everything with me. Everything on your mind. Everything on your heart.

He: Everything?

God: Yes. I won't be offended. Choose to be with me. I want to be with you.

[A minute goes by with nothing said.]

He: Would you tell me . . . who I am?

[After a while:]

God: You are mine.

He: *[Softly.]* I am?

God: *[A still, small voice.]* Yes. And I am yours.

[They are there, together . . . .]

FIRST REFLECTION:
"MEASURING THE DISTANCE"

"*I* don't even want to be with me!" Familiar? For many, Christians included, something like this statement would express the painful, often hidden truth about the way they think and feel about themselves. They do not like the person they are. They do not love themselves. The obvious must be stated: if I cannot endure being with me—if I am not a person I like to be around—this is not a sign of healthy self-love. We want to be with people we love.

There may be a lot of resistance to acknowledging the truth that we do not love ourselves—most of us believe that we *ought* to, so we put up a good front. But when we are alone . . . well, when we are alone *we are not alone.* That is the problem. There is a judge inside who sits with us . . . and there is so much evidence to sift!

It would be useful if we called this lack of self-love by its proper name. We are talking about self-hatred. If we say that we have self-hatred, that does not necessarily mean that hatred is the *only* thing we have for ourselves—we can and do harbor mutually contradictory things within our not yet fully converted hearts. It is just that we see so many things that are wrong with us. At times we feel like an illustration of Romans 7:15, "I do not understand what I do. For what I want to do I do not do, but what I hate I do."

But we do not stop with hating what we do and do not do. We hate the *doer*! And we hate the one who does *not* do. "Hate the sin, but love the sinner"? This is seldom our internal practice. We brood. We condemn. Our focus is on what is wrong with us. We are preoccupied with our shortcomings—with our sin.

There is something that we desperately need to know: God's ways are not our ways!

I remember a time, some years ago, when I sat brooding. Condemning. There was no doubt about it, the evidence was overwhelming: I was not doing what I thought I ought to be doing, and I was doing things that I hated. I berated myself. I told myself what a hopeless case I was. What a disappointment. "And I call myself a man of God?!" I kept running through my offenses again and again, squeezing from them every last drop of bitterness. The frustration was intense.

I do not remember exactly how it happened—I believe I had begun to offer this up as a cry to God—but at some point in this sad scene, God's word entered my mind. A warm and beautiful thought flowed into me, full of power: *"I am not counting your sins. I am measuring the distance."*

As the words were spoken in me, I understood their deepest meaning instantly in my heart. They came as a revelation of my heavenly Father's love. They drained wells of fear. They smashed jars of judgment. They swept open a narrow gate in a wall of the courtroom I was living in, and I came joyfully flooding out into the gift of the Father's loving mercy.

My heart understood. My mind was on the brink. I needed to open each phrase as a precious gift to be savored and understood more deeply.

"I am not counting your sins." I saw that I was preoccupied with my sin. God was not. The Father is not a law clerk sitting there at his desk recording my every transgression, making sure none are missed or forgotten, anxious that no misdeed goes unpunished through lack of scrupulous attention—appalled at the cumulative weight of it all! He's not sitting with beetled brow, shaking his head disapprovingly as the evidence mounts up and the list approaches that length where *something* will just *have* to be done.

He is not counting my sins. My ways are not his ways. It is not my sin that he cares about. He cares about me. *"I am measuring the distance."* Not the distance between me and the person I ought to be. Not the distance I need to go to measure up. What my Father measures is the distance between us.

We can know something of this. For instance, if we have suffered estrangement from a child—if we have seen our child going destructive ways and known the agony of a gulf widening between us. In the midst of this kind of loss, what do we measure? Do we keep track of her sins for a future reckoning? Or does our heart measure the distance and long for her return? When he comes near again do we point the finger, or do we reach out with open hands to draw him into our arms?

My Father measures the distance. When I return to him and he embraces me, I know that he has not been counting my sins. I feel the joy of his measuring heart.

This is not only how our Lord feels about me. This is how it is with your heavenly Father and you. He is not counting your sins. He is measuring the distance. His ways are not your ways.

A question might arise at this point: "Are you telling me that God doesn't give a hoot whether I sin or not?" No. I am not saying that. God cares very deeply. The question is, what does God care *about?*

Sometimes we act as though we believe God created moral laws just for the orneriness of it, or for the sport, or, perhaps, for the aesthetic joy he got from the beauty of those laws. And this god is really partial to his laws and dotes on them and is highly protective of them. Oh my, yes, and he gets offended *very* easily if so much as one little phrase is jostled. Even a minor infraction invites the back of his hand, or a wrathful memorizing for the day of our due. But, having dealt with us, this god turns back from us as quickly as possible to comfort his poor little law and he coos and murmurs his regret while casting barbed looks like spears at the cowering offender.

You will be relieved to know that the above description has nothing to do with the Christian faith, or with God. It is a description of an idol. Yet many of us live, to some extent, as though God were like that sick creature! We have reason to know better: this god does not even measure up to *human* standards!

If I tell a small child not to touch a pan-handle because it's hot and he goes ahead and touches it and is burned, I am concerned for the *child.* I may be upset, but not primarily because my law was broken. I am upset because the child is hurt. Healing is on my mind. And I want to help the child, in whatever way I can, to learn something from the experience that will be of value as he toddles on through the day and into tomorrow. Among other things, he may learn that there is love behind the law and that obedience has benefits!

The point is this: The Lord of Glory only does what love does: the law is an expression of the love of God, given as a *gift* to measure, inspire, convict, guide, and otherwise serve us.

When we sin, God's focus is not on some injury or offense done to the law, or even on the fact that we have broken the *law,* but rather on *the destructive consequences for us, for others, and for our relationship with him.* It was, after all, the *consequence* of sin—our spiritual death—that the Father saw and addressed in his Son who gave his life for us when the list of our sins was as long as death [Romans 5:8].

Why, then, *does* Jesus command us to forgive? It is *for our sake,* so that he can pour out the forgiveness in our hearts that we so desperately need. He forbids us to judge the worth of another human being because he does not want to see us come under the bondage and condemnation of that same judgment [Matthew 7:1ff]! Jesus commands us to love and forgive our enemies because he wants us to be like his Father—to have his heart—to be his sons and daughters [Matthew 5:43-48].

The commandments are portraits of God's children living faithfully in his Kingdom right here in this world. They are illustrations of the way we would behave if we were truly children of our heavenly Father. "Daughters" and "sons" would be like his only-begotten Son. In us, the law would be fulfilled through the obedience of love. Having received his love, we could and would love. We would love with his love . . . the love he shares with his Abba. Having received him into our hearts we would have self-giving love written there by the hand of the Holy Spirit.

"I am not counting your sins." I hope it is clear now that God is not indifferent to our sin. God is a perfect father—a perfect mother: he hates the sin, but he loves the sinner! God hates my sin because he knows its destructive effects on me and on many others. He hates the consequence of sin. But he loves the sinner, and he demonstrates that love, personally. There, in the toxic fallout from my sin, he meets me—broken, ashamed, condemned, and lost. There his merciful love shocks me into truth: it was I who counted my sins. It was I who went apart and sowed destruction in my life. Here in the wasteland of my sin, apart from him, I see the truth: in me, lawlessness is lovelessness!

If his commandment is an expression of his love, then when I break that commandment, I reject his love. But if I begin to make the connection between his commandment and his love, I come into the place of choosing. Will God's love for me remain unrequited, or will I accept his love and return it? If I choose to love him in return, I will need to walk in the light of a wonderful and difficult truth: *my choice to love him is a choice to obey him.*

When obedience to God's commandment comes, it is love's response to love offered. How could it be otherwise? How can I possibly believe that I love him if, at the same time, *I reject his love by disobeying him?* "You are God and I am going to love you but I am not going to do your will!" This is a spiritual oxymoron. Of course that is not the case if we turn it around and imagine God saying it to us: 'You are Sally May and I am going to love you, but I am not going to do your will!' Now *that* makes sense! As a matter of fact, God *does* say that continually (and not just to you, Sally May!)

It is true: a choice to love God is a choice to obey him. Therefore, our obedience to God is a perfectly accurate measure of our love of God. There is no gap between our love and our obedience. As Jesus said, *"Whoever has my commands and obeys them, he it is who loves me"* [John 14:21].

"Oh no, God," we say, *"anything* but that! I just want to be close to you and hear your comforting words of forgiveness and know that everything is going to be OK."

"Do you mean that you want to love me as my child?"

"Well, I mostly mean 'would you stop the bad things from happening', but, yes, sure, I want to be your child and love you."

"Loving me means obeying me, you know."

[Silence.] "OK, whatever it takes. I'll be a good child so you'll love me and protect me and the bad things will stop. OK?"

"But I have never stopped loving you. It is you who have not loved me. That is why both your hands are burned!"

[He looks down at the destruction.] "But I *do* love you!"

"To love me is to obey me, remember?"

"Right, but that's not working out. I try to obey, but my whole heart just isn't in it."

"Yes, the problem is there in your heart. You love many things more than you love me."

"Well can't you just fix my heart and make me love you more?"

"Compel you to obey me? Take away your freedom to choose to disobey?"

"Yes! Absolutely!"

"That is not an option. If you are to love me, then you must be free to choose me . . . or choose another way. Love without a choice is not love."

"Fine, then, I choose to love you."

"Fine, then, choose to obey me!"

And so we go round and round. And he continues to measure the distance.

But is God's insistence on obedience part of the way that he measures the distance? Yes, because we cannot obey unless we receive him as he draws near. We cannot obey him unless—through our nearness to him and by his transforming power—we *become* loving and therefore obedient persons! He measures the distance because he loves us and wants us near him, and because he knows that only in that closeness *to* him will we become *like* him.

Remember that the fellow in the previous dialogue had 'tried'. That means, of course, that he tried to keep the commandments. He is way ahead of many people—he knows he has failed. He thought that being obedient had only to do with trying harder. He tried to change his behavior and it wasn't working out. He ran up against the truth: obedience has to do with *being*—with who we are. Our doing comes from our being. Our words and our actions begin in our hearts [Matthew 5:28; 15:18ff]. It is for this reason that even if we are outwardly compliant to rules that is not synonymous with true obedience.

The problem is there in our hearts. We have chosen to love many things more than we love God. Jesus calls us back to the love foundation of eternal life with the commandment: "Love one another as I have loved you." This is first a call to obedient receptivity. We need to know the gift of the Father's love, in Jesus, before we can offer it back in response. The love we return results from a choice we make to receive that love by trusting the one who tells us who he is and who empowers us to come forth from our loveless tomb (the dark end of all disobedience) to the One who is love.

Jesus enters the darkness of our tomb. He comes as light into our lawless heart. As he is creatively present there, he offers us a new heart—one where love can find a home. As we accept the grace to receive it, his word of love makes us new.

"God demonstrates his own love for us in this: While we were still sinners, Christ died for us" [Romans 5:8].

His living word reaches deep into our hearts where we have known the devastation of lovelessness, inscribing there the law of love [Jeremiah 31:33]. There love abides. There, within us, he abides. And through our loving obedience, we abide in him. And we know the truth that it always was the *abiding* that was on God's mind and heart; that abiding was the point of every law, every act, every word—the point of all he does and does not do [John 15:9ff].

"I am not counting your sins. I am measuring the distance."

First Reflection In A Nutshell
"Measuring the Distance"

Here we see that intimacy with God is severely impeded by our false understanding of his nature and purposes. We can be shocked by the true dimensions of his love and by his desire to be with us, personally. There is a profound connection between the gift of God's law and the gift of his love. And yet God loves us, not his law. We see that our choice to respond in obedience to his law is our choice to receive and respond to the love he offers. God addresses the consequences of our sin by his reconciling word of love spoken in his Son.

Questions for reflection or discussion

1. "Hate the sin, but love the sinner": is it possible to love the sinner and at the same time "love" the sin? In terms of my relationship with myself, could a lack of hatred for my sin be one way that I do not effectively love myself?

2. To be "preoccupied with my sin" does not necessarily mean that I sit around saying "I've sinned, I've sinned, I've sinned!" I may just feel depressed. What are other forms this preoccupation might take? How does it look in you?

3. Reflect on these statements: "My preoccupation with my disobedience is one way that I avoid obedience: I beat myself up to avoid repentance."

4. Given that we do sin, what is the alternative to beating ourselves up over it or being preoccupied with it?

5. Do you believe that it is not your sin "but the consequences of your sin that God cares about"? Do your feelings and/or your actions always reflect that belief? When they don't, what belief do they reflect?

MEDITATION ON PSALM 14
"The fool says in his heart, 'there is no God'"

"There is no God." This is a kind of "code" phrase and requires translation. Several are possible, but the most common key to translation, in my experience, is found in the place of pain and anger where unexamined words came to life: "there is no God" began as "I hate God." The "code" is broken there in the broken heart where it began. "I hate God" is spoken within the context of a relationship with God ("I hate *you*"), be it ever so immature and unexamined and falsely founded. Now, in revenge for what may be perceived as injustice, a new word is spoken, which is an attempt to dismiss (along with the relationship) the very existence of the offender: "there is no God." This is attempted murder. The defendant will make a bitter plea of self-defense:

"This so-called-god left us unprotected. He took my child from me. I am told that this god of love did it in order to teach me something. I hate the god I thought there was!"

And I want to cry out, "yes! You are right to reject the god who is not God. There is a living God. He made you; he loves you, he is for you, and after you. Go after him. Go back to 'I hate *you*': the God who is God will meet you there!"

Where am I in this? You know, Jesus, that there was an extended time when I entertained the thought "there is no God." For me there was a different translation; those words meant, "I want to do what I want to do." I was not entertaining innocence. This was no serious search for truth. It was simply that in order for me to do what I wanted to do, I could not know what I knew. "There is no God" became a life-style, but it never was anything I believed. I did (before and after all) know what I knew.

Do I still live the lifestyle called "there is no God"? I'm asking you, Jesus.

"In the places where you persist in choosing your will over mine, it is necessary for you not to know what you know. When you choose not to know what you know, you choose not to know me. There are things in you that can only have life if you put me to death."

I want your loving life, Jesus. I want your obedient life. I want to put to death anything that blocks your Way in me. I say this to you, the living God: "You Are! I choose your death. I choose your life. I choose your power. I choose to know what I know!"

SCRIPTURAL SCENE:
"THE RICH MAN AND LAZARUS"

Luke 16:19-31

"There was a rich man who was dressed in purple and fine linen and lived in luxury every day. At his gate was laid a beggar named Lazarus, covered with sores and longing to eat what fell from the rich man's table. Even the dogs came and licked his sores.

The time came when the beggar died and the angels carried him to Abraham's side. The rich man also died and was buried. In hell, where he was in torment, he looked up and saw Abraham far away, with Lazarus by his side. So he called to him, 'Father Abraham, have pity on me and send Lazarus to dip the tip of his finger in water and cool my tongue, because I am in agony in this fire.'

But Abraham replied, 'Son, remember that in your lifetime you received your good things, while Lazarus received bad things, but now he is comforted here and you are in agony. And besides all this, between us and you a great chasm has been fixed, so that those who want to go from here to you cannot, nor can anyone cross over from there to us.'

He answered, 'Then I beg you, father, send Lazarus to my father's house, for I have five brothers. Let him warn them, so that they will not also come to this place of torment.'

Abraham replied, 'They have Moses and the Prophets; let them listen to them.'

No, father Abraham,' he said, 'but if someone from the dead goes to them, they will repent.'

He said to him, 'If they do not listen to Moses and the Prophets, they will not be convinced even if someone rises from the dead.'"

SECOND REFLECTION:
"CHOOSING GOD'S WORD"

In the story of the rich man and Lazarus, Jesus brings us a profound teaching on the role of human choice in receiving the word of God. He speaks a truth which exposes an ageless human delusion: "If God would speak to me in a powerful and unmistakable way, then I would accept it as his word and obey without question."

This deception primarily concerns the human side of the equation—it embodies a fatal misreading of the depth of the rebellion in the human heart—but just beneath the surface is a complaint against God that goes something like this: "The main roadblock concerning my communication with God is that he has a real problem with voice projection—he is so far away and his voice doesn't quite reach me most of the time. He needs to speak up and be clear!"

I believe that these companion delusions were a major ingredient in the demand for 'signs' that Jesus responded to with unequivocal censure during his earthly ministry. The relentless insistence on signs put Jesus in mind of Jonah:

> *"A wicked and adulterous generation asks for a miraculous sign! But none will be given it except the sign of the prophet Jonah. For as Jonah was three days and three nights in the belly of a huge fish, so the Son of Man will be three days and three nights in the heart of the earth. The men of Nineveh will stand in judgment with this generation and condemn it; for they repented at the preaching of Jonah, and now one greater than Jonah is here".*
>
> [Matthew 12:39-40]

Yet Jesus' whole ministry was characterized by wonderful signs—why rebuke those who were interested in them? I believe it was because Jesus knew that those who *demanded* signs were not really interested in receiving anything from God, especially not a call to repentance. Because they had no intention of receiving the word he was bringing them in the flesh, those Jesus rebuked would not have received that word through any means of expression be it ever so powerful or, supposedly, irresistible. He knew that. He knew their delusions and deceptions. And Jesus knew that signs could be discounted and ignored no matter how spectacular. In themselves, they could not produce faith apart from a willingness to see and to hear and to choose [John 12:37-40]!

Jesus unmasks our rebellion and delusions in the parable of the rich man and Lazarus. The rich man had ignored poor, suffering Lazarus at his doorstep. He may have tithed but he did not love. He may have kept the dietary laws but he did not act on God's word, clearly there in Hebrew scripture, that should have lead him to have compassion on Lazarus who starved at his gate.

So the rich man finds himself in hell, suffering, and, because there is no other remedy, he asks Abraham to make the truth clear to his relatives—to warn them so that they will not come to the same suffering end he has come to. In effect, he is saying this: "I was listening all my life for your voice, God, but you were speaking below the range of human hearing. All I had was Moses in a book. If you had just made your voice loud enough and clear enough I would have obeyed, and if you will just speak the truth to my brothers loudly and clearly enough, they will do the right thing. Send Lazarus. He'll come to them express from heaven! Surely they'll listen to him because they'll be able to see and hear him"!

There is every reason to assume that the rich man was exposed to God's written word all his life (Jesus implies this when he states that the brothers "have Moses"). But, obviously, God's word has made no progress in his heart. He does not know his heart or his brothers' hearts. He is deluded. And we can hear in his solution echoes of the tired old complaint about God's incompetence as a communicator.

Jesus uncovers the deception and the delusions and teaches that we human beings can hear God's word and not receive it. We can live alongside God's word and never let it in. We can know every word of the Word and still remain untouched by it. How is this possible? What is missing in the one who does not receive?

I remember a day some years ago when I was sitting in the church where I was serving, worshipping and praying for that church and its life. Then a very common and ordinary thing happened: the Holy Spirit spoke to me. I recognize that for many people this type of statement can present a major problem. We have heard such things before: "Yesterday God said to me, he said, Ralph, I'll tell you what I want you to do. At 3:30 this afternoon I want you to get up and get in your car and drive out to Bertha's place and tell her in no uncertain terms . . ."(and so forth). This can be hard to take! Part of the reason is that those who say things like that about God speaking to them in that way never describe what they *mean* by it. What did they actually experience? We do a lot of assuming. We end up believing that God speaks very rarely (if at all) and only to the special few selected for the privilege. And we are very sure that we are not one of them.

With that in mind, I am going to try to describe what I actually experienced. Using some scripture as the foundation (Ephesians 3:14-19, to be exact), I was praying for the church. Then God spoke to me. I did not hear an audible voice. It is important to point out that God does still speak to his people in an audible voice on occasion, as well as in dreams, visions, inner thoughts and feelings, other people, etc, and always and most importantly in scripture. However, as I said, I did not hear an audible voice, but suddenly, right in the middle of my prayer, I knew something. I had a clear, strong thought: I "knew" that we (members of that church) were being invited to receive an infilling of the Holy Spirit at a gathering that was already planned for an evening in the near future. Right away I also knew (another unbidden thought) that I was to pray for that infilling at the gathering. As soon as I had that thought I responded instantly by praying for it right then. The words streamed out with no effort or thought on my part. I knew that the Holy Spirit was praying in me. (When I was done I could remember almost none of it, so the Holy Spirit would have to pray in and through me again at the gathering! Scary stuff . . . I would have to trust him!)

Now here is the question: how was I sure that what I heard (suddenly knew) was of God? The answer is this: I wasn't sure . . . not *absolutely* sure!

This has happened many, many times in my life. Suddenly I have a thought; suddenly I have known, or seen, or felt, or just sensed something. I have chosen to believe that what I experienced was God speaking to me. Then I have chosen to actively respond to what I have heard. That usually involves some element of risky trust. I have noticed the results that come from this scary obedience. What I have learned is that when I allow the things that I believe God is saying to me to affect what I say and do, things happen! Sometimes these things that result are little, sometimes bigger and more dramatic, but they are always things that I know I did not plan or empower, and they always come as life and blessing. Sometimes the things which happen as a result of my obedience to God's word cause me (and/or others) to experience some kind of suffering, but I know that such suffering is simply the way God's life and blessing come that day.

For example, if I tell you that I see something operating in you that is destructive, and that I believe Jesus desires to touch that place, your response to that information could result in a difficult, even painful time for you—it is hard to face the truth sometimes and to work through it with Jesus. But in the long run, it will be a wonderful time: freedom from that destructiveness is life and blessing for you.

Of course, I have had to learn to recognize God's voice in my life. This is not a given and it does not happen overnight. It requires perseverance, and it involves *choices*! You may have noticed that I said I "chose" to believe that what I thought, felt, saw, etc., was from God. *I had a choice!* It would have been possible to turn away from the knowing, or feeling, or seeing—to talk myself out of it one way or another. The person in the example above could have done the same. At first he might have sensed the truth of what was said. But if it then occurred to him that a difficult time would follow for him if he received that truth as a word from God, he might have ended up rejecting what I had said to him as nothing more than a critical, spiteful word from me! "I didn't know you felt *that* way about me. I thought you were my *Pastor*, not my *enemy*!" God speaks to us often through other people, but if we are not alert to that possibility and committed to hearing him in that way, we may not "have ears to hear."

And there are many other ways we can turn a deaf ear to God's word in our lives. For example, we might think, "I had that thought but it couldn't possibly have been from God because God doesn't talk to ordinary people." Or we may reject God's word because we suspect that if we accepted that it really *was* from God then we would have to do something we hadn't planned on—something risky—something that would cost us some effort and, perhaps, make us look foolish. Sometimes our pride stands in the way.

Other times it is judgment that inhibits us: if we judge others who have the audacity to believe that God speaks to them, we will probably assume that that same judgment will be visited on us (*we* will certainly visit it on us!) should we claim that he has spoken to us: "If I say that I believe this is a word from God then they're going to say 'well, who does she think *she* is pretending that God talks to her'"!

Hear this, please: God is never going to speak to you in a way that makes your need to choose unnecessary. Granted, his voice can be more or less resistible! But even when God speaks so powerfully that it "breaks the Cedars of Lebanon" we can almost immediately begin to talk ourselves out of ever having heard him, becoming convinced within a week that it was any number of other things including our hyperactive imagination acting up again.

Or we might reject it by refusing to move in obedient response to that word. This too is a failure to choose. In effect we say, "That's God's word but it has nothing to do with me"! Choosing God's word means more than choosing to believe that it *is* God's word.

I remember going to dances as a boy (in the middle of the last century) where we began with the girls lined up on one side of the dance floor and the boys on the other. When the excitedly anticipated and fearfully dreaded hour was ripe, some giddy adult would cheerfully yell something like "All right gentlemen, get over there and choose your partner!" Many painful, exciting, disappointing, shaming, joy-filled, embarrassing things could happen at this point, but let's look at it in the friendliest light possible and suppose that the girl who inspires my almost-lethal heart palpitations is still there when I arrive on the other side and she is actually glad to see me approaching. I say "May I have the honor of the . . . I mean would you care if . . . could we . . . uh . . . would . . . uh . . ." and she says, smiling, "sure!", being adept at translating masculine, dance-decision-drivel by this time, and I take her hand (thereby losing almost all functional consciousness) as we head for the middle of the dance floor.

Now this is what choosing looks like! Nothing less will do. If I approach the young lady and say "Well I'm here and that's really you and this is really exciting . . . bye now!" and walk away to someone else, then as far as my choosing the girl in question is concerned, this falls a bit short. I may be deluded into thinking I have chosen her, but here is the test: as I walk away, would *she* say that she has been chosen?

So I have not completed choosing God's word simply because I have chosen to believe that this thought I have had, or this word I have read, etc, is God's word. Important as that choice is, it is only the equivalent of my saying, "well I'm here and that's really you, God, and this is really exciting." I haven't completed choosing God's word until my hand is in his and we're dancing.

First I choose to believe that this word God is speaking is for me, personally, and I receive his word in my heart. Now my hand is in his. Then

I choose to examine my life in its light and I begin to choose to respond in obedience—concretely—to his word in me. Now we're dancing.

Unless we understand the necessity of choosing God's word, we are apt to believe any number of lies about ourselves, and (especially) about God. I described two ancient deceptions earlier. Another very common one is this: "Because of who I am, God can't speak to me. It is all my fault. I try to listen but I never 'get' anything because God has given up on me, and I probably didn't try hard enough anyway, which God can't endure, so he stops talking in disgust." This lie appears to be a belief about who I am, but it may reveal more about who I believe God to be. What sort of a view of God does this present? Poor God: he created the universe but he can't get through to me. And he's petulant, and petty.

We must acknowledge that this false understanding can be there in spite of some genuine attempts to listen to God and to hear his word—efforts that have met with little or no apparent success. This could be the result of our having adopted a passive posture relative to God's word—a stance that is totally at odds with the nature of the relationship he calls us to. It is within the context of an intimate relationship that he calls us to hear and respond to his voice.

Jesus does not invite us into a relationship in which we passively have things done to us. Our progress into intimacy with the Father is furthered by receptivity, not passivity. The primary difference between the two comes in the area of the engagement of my will. When I am passive, things "happen to me." I can remain completely disconnected from the source of what is happening: in this case, God. Because God's eternal word is always about relationship [John 17:3], it cannot be received passively. Passivity is not the stuff of intimate relationship—not the stuff of relationship at all—rather it is a protective barrier against it. When I am passive, I do not have to be open for receiving or giving. I do not have to be vulnerable. The things that happen to me happen outside my will, without my choosing them, so I reserve my right to disavow any responsibility for, or association with, anything that follows as a consequence. Passivity is the stuff of disconnection. It serves estrangement.

When I am receptive, I am engaged, actively and vulnerably, with the one who comes to give and to receive. I don't just stand there and "take it," I choose. Jesus is our model: he was not the passive victim of people who took his life from him. He chose to give his life—to lay it down for us [John 10:17-18].

Now we can see what was missing in the rich man who lived with the word of God through Moses: though he lived with the word of God very near him, he never chose it. He stood passively alongside the word. Certainly he may have done all kinds of things that looked active in response to that word—he may have been a scrupulous observer of the letter of the law. But he would have confined his 'choosing' and his "obeying"—all his action—to some selected external things only. He would have done some of the outward things, but only in order to make it easier to fend off the word and prevent it from affecting his heart. He never chose to receive the word inwardly. His heart was safe from the word of costly compassion. I have no doubt he knew the compassionate word of scripture and that he believed it was from God. "I'm really here and that's really you in your word, Lord," he would say, "and I'm really excited about the compassion thing (I weep when I hear it)." But he did not know the feel of his Father's hand, and he did not know the steps of choosing that lead to life.

How wonderful that Jesus has lived and spoken the truth: there is always going to be a choice that must be made. The obedience God requires of me is never going to be the result of God overpowering my will with his own, as though his irresistible Word has finally been delivered and I'm swept up beyond my ability to run from it. It is important that we do not underestimate the sinfulness and rebellion of our hearts: in this life, you and I will always have the capacity to turn away from *any* truth, including the One who *is* Truth. That will remain the case until judgment day. If you do not chose to believe and to act on the tiny, still, mistakable voice that comes to you today, then, in spite of whatever delusions you may harbor, you are not going to believe even a cedar-shattering thunderbolt of a voice. *Even if that voice comes from one who has risen from the dead.*

It is only as we choose to respond to that still, small, very mistakable voice that we grow in our capacity to know his voice more clearly and personally. Sometimes I am amazed at just how small and faint the communication is that I respond to, and act from, much of the time—so soft that years ago much of it would have gone unnoticed by me.

If you believe that God does not or cannot speak to you, then you are deceived. You have believed an old, convenient and comfortable lie. You need to know the truth: God is bringing his living word to you. It may be that you are waiting for God to speak to you in exactly the same way you assume he speaks to others, who may talk as though there was no choice made and none needed. But there was and there is. It may be that you are not aware that when God communicates with you it is vitally important that you believe it is God's voice and that you respond in some active way.

Because the Father loves us he has given us the freedom to choose. By his grace, you can and must choose. You can choose Jesus and love him by choosing to believe that his living words are for you, and by choosing to receive and obey them, whether they are in the form of a thought that comes, or his written word, or an audible voice; whether whispering or tree-busting!

Please: don't put off choosing until the last Trumpet sounds. If what you yearn for is something you can be *absolutely* sure about, well, that last trumpet call will be unmistakable and irresistible. But the time for choosing will have ended.

Speak precious Lord, your servants choose to listen.

Second Reflection: In A Nutshell
"Choosing his Word"

Jesus uncovers our deceptions and the delusions and teaches that we human beings can hear God's word and not receive it. We can live alongside God's word and never let it in. We can know every word of the Word and still remain untouched by it. We can choose Jesus and love him by choosing to believe that his living words are for us, and by choosing to receive and obey them, whether they are in the form of a thought that comes, or his written word, or an audible voice; whether whispering or tree-busting!

Questions for reflection or discussion

1. Do you sometimes believe this: "If God would speak to me in a powerful and unmistakable way, then I would accept it as his word and obey without question"? Reflect on this in the light of Matthew 25:21, "Well done, good and faithful servant! You have been faithful with a few things; I will put you in charge of many things."

2. Do you envy those who seem to get loud and clear communication from God? Would you be willing to confess this to God and ask for forgiveness? If so, do so. If not, why not? What do you think Jesus would want you to understand and what gift would he give you to replace the envy?

3. Which of these statements would best express the attitude of your heart toward God on a typical day: (a) "I want so many things and I'm trusting in you to provide them"; or (b) "I want to know and do your will"? Are these equally important? Are they mutually exclusive? What impact would a shift in primary focus from (a) to (b) have on your listening for and response to God's voice?

4. Reflect on anything which you believe may be God's word to you in the recent past. Where are you in relation to choosing that word? Have you chosen to believe that these thoughts you have had, or words you have read, etc, really are God's word? Have you said, in effect, "well I'm here and that's really you, God, and this is

really exciting"? Have you moved further along? Is "your hand in his"? Are you "dancing"?

5. Reflect on choosing God's Word in the light of the fact that Jesus has come all the way across the dance floor to you and chosen you! Allow yourself to picture him coming to you that way. Dance with him! Some men may want to picture Jesus as captain of the 'team'. It's time to choose players from among all those standing around. He and the other leader will take turns choosing until the teams are complete. Jesus will choose first. You have no hope, but, incredibly, he looks at you. It's clear that he wants you on his side. He calls you by name and you come to stand proudly near him: the first chosen!

MEDITATION ON PSALM 11
"In the Lord have I taken refuge;
How can they say to me, 'fly away like a bird'."

It is certain that I'm hunted. Creatures of the hunter beat the bushes hoping to scare something up. They hope I'll fly away exposed. They hope for a clear shot: they want to pierce my heart.

As my world shudders and sways everything in me wants to lift off. Fear sees a place, just beyond these branches, where there is neither turmoil nor violence (so it seems)—a place of clear sky and no thrashing. "Go, go, go!" a voice in me cries out. "Lift yourself up! Leave this trembling world and fly to that safe place so clearly there beyond the shaking branches of this Tree."

Then Truth blows through me (another Voice) and I turn. Yes Lord! I know the truth. I may feel fear, but I know your love. I may be swaying, but I'm sober! I know the truth. This is my Father's Kingdom Tree. This Tree is rooted in Rock, and watered by eternal springs. This Tree reaches to the heavens in praise. This Tree is the garden Tree whose name is "Life"!

Having been lured from the empty sky by your love, Father, having settled here (perched in Paradise) I'll stay, thank you very much! Let evil arrows fly: my heart is here in you, so I'll perch, praise you very much!

SCRIPTURAL SCENE:
"I TELL YOU THE TRUTH."

Mark 14:26-42

When they had sung a hymn, they went out to the Mount of Olives.

"You will all fall away," Jesus told them, "for it is written: 'I will strike the shepherd, and the sheep will be scattered.'

But after I have risen, I will go ahead of you into Galilee."

Peter declared, "Even if all fall away, I will not."

"I tell you the truth," Jesus answered, "today—yes, tonight—before the rooster crows twice you yourself will disown me three times."

But Peter insisted emphatically, "Even if I have to die with you, I will never disown you." And all the others said the same.

They went to a place called Gethsemane, and Jesus said to his disciples, "Sit here while I pray." He took Peter, James and John along with him, and he began to be deeply distressed and troubled. "My soul is overwhelmed with sorrow to the point of death," he said to them. "Stay here and keep watch."

Going a little farther, he fell to the ground and prayed that if possible the hour might pass from him. "Abba, Father," he said, "everything is possible for you. Take this cup from me. Yet not what I will, but what you will."

Then he returned to his disciples and found them sleeping. "Simon," he said to Peter, "are you asleep? Could you not keep watch for one hour? Watch and pray so that you will not fall into temptation. The spirit is willing, but the body is weak."

Once more he went away and prayed the same thing. When he came back, he again found them sleeping, because their eyes were heavy. They did not know what to say to him.

Returning the third time, he said to them, "Are you still sleeping and resting? Enough! The hour has come. Look, the Son of Man is betrayed into the hands of sinners. Rise! Let us go! Here comes my betrayer!"

THIRD REFLECTION:
"CHOOSING TO KNOW AND TO BE KNOWN"

This profoundly moving scene is a record of the final private moments between Jesus and his disciples. It is the last scene of their earthly communion. Jesus spoke to his followers only one more time after this—brief words from the cross to his mother and to John. And after this time in Gethsemane there are only a few scattered words addressed by disciples to him before his death: those spoken by his followers expressing their willingness to use swords when the rulers come to arrest him and the curse from the lips of his betrayer that came in the guise of a greeting: "Rabbi"! Nor was he touched again in *love* by a disciple, but only by Judas who drew close to deliver him up by a kiss of death.

This short time on the Mount of Olives is a treasure for us—a gift of sight. Here in the garden we see the One who came to open a human way to intimacy with The Father. We see him living out that intimacy in these last hours with his disciples and friends.

For Jesus, intimacy with God The Father meant knowing and being known [Luke 10:22]. This mutual knowing and being known was the river of eternal life they shared, whose source was continual, mutual, self-revealing, self-giving love. It was this eternal life of loving that Jesus shared with the disciples. "As the Father has loved me," he told them, "so have I loved you" [John 15:9].

The Father, because it is the desire of his heart and because he loves his Son, opens himself to be known. The Son, because it is the desire of his heart and because he loves his Father, opens *himself* to be known.

Jesus, then, *lives* and *offers* this way of life for his followers. A king does not share his heart with the servant who washes his feet, but Jesus, King of kings and Lord of lords, the Anointed One, the Savior, the Son of God, desires to be known by his disciples—he shares his mind and heart with them. And *he* washes *their* feet. He opens himself and shares himself with them as he does with the Father. When Philip asks Jesus to show them the Father, Jesus says, *"Have you been with me this long and you still do not know me Phillip?"* [John 14:9] If they do not know him, it is not for lack of opportunity. He withholds nothing from them that they can bear [John 16:12].

Jesus in his perfect humanity is perfectly free to be who he is and to share himself with us so that we can know him and know the Father. Never is this more apparent than in this final day with his disciples. Here Jesus shares his deepest agony. Both his willingness and his freedom to do this reveal the perfection of his humanity and his sacrificial love. He does not share his struggle in hindsight—not from the relatively safe vantage point of resolution or victory. To his closest friends he submits the raw, jagged, unfinished writhing of his suffering heart, mind and body. "My soul is overwhelmed with sorrow to the point of death . . . ." He withholds nothing of himself from them. This is the riskiest, deepest, most personal, most *human* offering possible.

But Jesus does more than open himself to be known by the disciples. As he reveals his heart, he reveals the Father's heart. He had been explicit with Phillip: *"He who has seen me has seen the Father. How can you say, 'Show us the Father'?"* As Jesus is, so God the Father is. In Jesus we see that it is God's desire to be known. The Father opened his heart and mind—his *life*—to us when he sent his Son to be the Word of Truth about himself, spoken to us in human flesh. He opened himself to be known because that is what love does. And he reveals himself for *our* sake because, for us, knowing him *is* life.

This is the fulfillment of God's will for humankind: in and through our Savior, Jesus, we can know God! [Jeremiah 31:33-34] It cannot be said too often: this knowing *is* eternal life!

Jesus said that Eternal Life *is* knowing God and knowing the One sent by God (Jesus) [John 17:3]. But what does it mean to 'know God'? Does it simply mean that we know things *about* God? Scripture does speak of knowing in that way. We could say, with Paul, that all human kind has "known" God from the beginning, because "God's invisible qualities—his eternal power and divine nature—have been clearly seen, being understood from what has been made . . ." [Romans 1:20]. Paul is explicit: the "knowing" he describes is knowing "about", or "of"[v.19]. Information about God is important but Paul's point in this passage is that this kind of knowing was and is not enough in itself: it must lead to another kind of knowing.

The people Paul refers to fall short of the mark: "They neither glorified him as God, nor gave thanks to him . . . ." Our knowing about God begins when God reveals himself, but its fulfillment is found in the response of the human heart to the One who opens himself to be known. *Response* is necessary if "knowing about" is to move into the deeper "knowing" that is eternal life. It was this personal response that was lacking in those people who "knew" God through the wonder of God's creation.

I repeat: the people Paul refers to knew God because he chose to reveal himself to them. Creation was, in truth, a personal word spoken to all people, but those who acknowledged *only* the word (the creation) thereby rejected the One who spoke the word (the Creator). It was as though they were saying "I do not want to know you, I only want to know *about* you." This is always a fatal choice. When knowledge about God does not lead to the deeper knowing that grows up from a thankful and submitted heart, then the "knowledge about" becomes like a seed that rots in the ground. No life comes from it. Hidden away from the One who is Light, it twists and distorts, conforming itself to the shapes and ways of darkness and death [vv. 21-25]. Ultimately, that knowledge about God which is lodged in a resolutely unsubmitted heart is no more life giving than that held by demons who "believe and shudder" [James 2:19; cf. Mark 1:24, 34].

What, then, is the "knowing" that is eternal life? For the answer we must turn to Jesus, who tells us that he is "the Way, the Truth, and the Life" [John 14:6]. I believe that one of the levels of meaning in these three truths about Jesus concerns "knowing". He is the *Truth* that we can know about the Father. He is also the *Way* to knowing the Father. And when Jesus says that he is the *Life*, he means that the way in which he knows the Father must be our way if we are to know as he does and *live*.

The simple truth is that *in order to know as Jesus knows we must love as he loves*. We have seen this already: his knowledge of the Father comes in the context of their mutual, self-revealing, self-giving love. This is deeply responsive love. There is no other kind. Jesus never treats the Father's word or will as information to be gathered and dispensed. When the Father gives his word, he gives himself. Therefore, when Jesus receives the Father's word he receives him. It is not just his word, but the Father himself who abides in Jesus. And he is the Responsive Word of Love, abiding in the Father [John 14:10ff].

To know the Father as Jesus knows him is to know him through loving him. Listen to John, the disciple "whom Jesus loved": "everyone who loves is born of God and knows God. Whoever does not love does not know God, because God is love [1John 4:7b-8]." We enter into abiding intimacy with the Father through love: "Whoever lives in love lives in God, and God in him [1 John 4:16c]."

Responsive, abiding love: this is the pathway of the "knowing" which is eternal life. Yet we may still ask, "Exactly *how* does love respond? By what *means* can I abide? How is this love *expressed*?" All the answers are in Jesus: ". . . through the obedience of the one man [Jesus] the many will be made righteous [Romans 5:19b]." In him we see that the hallmark of a genuinely loving response to the living God is *obedience*. This is the foundation of a "righteous (right) relationship" with God. The obedience of love brought Jesus to the garden of Gethsemane. Jesus made it clear that this way of obedience, which he pioneered, would have to be our way if we were to have a life-giving knowledge of God. Jesus speaks the truth. We can only love God (and love Jesus) through obeying him: "If you obey . . . you will remain (abide) . . ."! And again, "If anyone loves me he will obey my teaching [John 14:23]."

Therefore: *In order to know as Jesus knows we must obey as he obeys.* His Way is not a way *around* obedience for us. It is the Way *into* the obedience that lies at the heart of intimacy with God: "If you obey my commandments, you will remain [abide] in my love, just as I have obeyed my Father's commands and remain [abide] in his love [John 15:10]." In terms of our relationship with God, *our obedience is love's response to love offered*. Listen to the beloved disciple: "The man who says 'I know him', but does not do what he commands is a liar . . . but if anyone obeys his word, God's love is truly made complete in him. This is how we know that we are in him: whoever claims to live in him must walk as Jesus did" [1 John 2:4–6]. Note the chain of connection: knowing is loving is obeying is living ("in him")! Knowledge of God leads to life!

Jesus walks the way of knowing the Father—of abiding intimacy. He walks in obedience. Jesus never says, "I only want to know about you—I do not want to know you." He is never disobedient. The hand of disobedience pushes the Father away. Disobedience refuses to know the One who has opened himself to be known. Disobedience refuses to respond to the Word by receiving the One who speaks.

This, I believe, was the disobedient path of Judas, who betrayed Jesus. Judas refused to open his heart and allow Jesus to come in. He would not be cleansed by him; he would not be fed by him; he refused to know him or be known by him. The seed of truth *about* Jesus, sown in the heart of Judas, rotted there and became the twisted root of a plant whose fruit was betrayal and death.

But before Jesus and the disciples entered the garden, Jesus identified a kind of betrayal that can only rise from a heart where true knowing has lived. He spoke these words to Peter: ". . . . tonight before the rooster crows twice you yourself will disown me three times." And so he did. One of the few who really knew Jesus "disowned" him. One has to have "owned" him first if one is to "disown" him. One cannot lose what one has never had.

What kind of suffering is it to experience the *loss of Jesus*? No wonder Peter's words of betrayal dissolved into bitter tears. I believe that Peter could not have survived the horrendous consequences of such a betrayal without the perfect intercession of the one whom he betrayed [Luke 22:31ff]. After all, it is one thing to say of a person, "I no longer believe that *about* him", when you do not know him. It is entirely another thing to say, "I do not know him", when you do. The agony that followed for Peter must have come as an experience of estrangement—of devastating loss. But in that place of denial, it was horribly true: he did not know him. The experience of that lack of knowing was an experience of death itself for Peter.

Yet in looking at Peter we can see that to deny knowing Jesus in a moment of time is not the same thing as not knowing him at all. *It was true that Peter did not know this Suffering Jesus—he was still determined not to know the Messiah whose life ends on a cross* [Matthew16:21-22]. But Peter's fleshly tongue uttered a lie nonetheless, because this truth was not the *whole* truth! His willing spirit spoke this fuller truth with tears of sadness, remorse and longing . . . . Peter wept. Though it would take the living water of the Spirit's indwelling to bring Kingdom fruit, it is clear that the seed of eternal knowing was rooted in Peter's responsive, yielded heart.

As a true disciple of Jesus, Peter had seen and experienced the Way of intimacy; of giving and receiving; of knowing and being known. Peter learned from Jesus in order to become like him. He did not withhold himself from Jesus in expressing his desire to be fearless and faithful "Even if all fall away, I will not". And Peter did not withhold himself when he turned back from his betrayal, yielding, through tears, the truth of who he was—the fearful brokenness of his heart—to the Father.

In Peter as in Jesus we see that the obedient responsiveness of love includes a willingness to be known. If our obedient love begins with receiving the One who desires to be known (for our sake!), it is completed in a responsive offering of all that we are to the One who has come very near in order that we also can be known. And so we come to this: *we cannot know as we must unless we are willing to be known.* Here we enter a stunning but beautiful truth. It will be worth whatever it takes to grasp and to live the truth that, in order to have life, *we need to be known.*

We begin by seeing this truth in Jesus, who does not speak of knowing his Father without at the same time speaking of his being known *by* the Father. It is no different when he refers to our eternal relationship with him: knowing and being known are inseparable [John 10:14-15].

This is hard for us. We may understand that we need to know as Jesus knows, *but what of our being known by God?* Is it possible that our being known by God depends upon our *willingness* to be known? *Surely we are known by God whether or not we desire it!* It would seem obvious that being known by God simply comes with the human territory! God knows every*thing* perfectly; every*one* comprehensively: you, me—all his creatures—then, now and forever. He knew us before we were born [Jeremiah 1:5], he knew us perfectly in forming us in our mother's womb; there is no place we can go where he will not know everything about us [Psalm 139:1-14], including our needs [Matthew 6:8], the thoughts of our mind [Psalm 94:11], and the truths of our heart [Luke 16:15]. John provides the exclamation point: ". . . he knows everything [1John 3:20c]"!

But we have seen that there is a knowing which is eternal life and there is a knowing which is knowing *about.* We have seen that there is a way that we can know God which is simply knowing *about* God. We must look again at the difference between "knowing" and "knowing about" and then we need to see how those truths apply to God's knowledge of us.

We begin with the basic truth: to know *about* someone is not the same thing as knowing them. If I know someone, I have a personal r*elationship* with them—this is an indispensable part of knowing them.

"Do you know where the President was born?"

"Yes."

"Do you know where he went to school?"

"Yes"

"Do you know where he lives."

"Sure."

"Great! Let's go! I want you to introduce me to him."

"O dear!"

"What's the problem?"

"Well . . . I don't really know him in that way."

"How *do* you know him?"

"Ahh . . . well I don't actually *know* him at all. I don't have a relationship with him—I've never met him. I just know some things about him. If we show up at his door, we'll be turned away! He doesn't know me."

I can know *about* God. But that is not a *relational* knowing and, therefore, does not mean that I know him in the Eternal Way. But as far as relational knowing goes, things work both ways. First, we cannot know the Father unless he opens himself to be known. God chooses to open himself to me and share himself with me in order that I can have life. Second, we cannot be "known" by the Father unless we open ourselves to be known. I receive the life he offers by receiving him and by making the same choice to be known.

The choice must be mutual if I am to have a life-giving relationship with God. It is not enough that we know *about* God. And it is not enough that God knows *about* us!

Our awareness of God's omniscience can actually blind us to the truth! It is easy for us to see that knowing the President's hat size does not usher us into the circle of those who know him and have a relationship with him. It is much harder for us to think in relational terms when we think of God toward us. But the truth is that the capacity to know, as God does, the inner thoughts of a man, or his feelings, yearnings, motives, or memories, is no different in *kind* than the capacity to know when he had lunch or what size hat he wears. All of it is information *about* the man. The amount of information we can know depends upon our capacity to gather it.

God has the capacity to know everything about any human being—external or internal. And he does know everything. Most of us acknowledge this. But what we infer from it leads to a sadly misinformed turn away from intimacy with God. "God knows about me" is automatically equated with "God knows me." This leaves our hearts untouched. This keeps God at a safe distance. This is not the way of love and that is a problem because love is the key to knowing *and* to being known. If we desire to come into the place of intimacy, we must come to see that the issues of intimacy are always issues of love.

We have seen that love is the key to our knowing God. Can it be any surprise that love is the key to our being known by God? In creating us in love, for love, God has placed himself within the limitations of the Way of love (or we could simply say, "he is who he is"!): if we will not love him he cannot know us. Paul states it positively: "The man who loves God is known by God!" [1 Cor. 8:3] In the same way that Paul recognizes a human knowledge "about" God, he is fully aware that God has comprehensive knowledge *about* us. But he directs us to that "knowing" which is eternal life.

This is where Jesus directs and leads us. When we understand the place of "knowing" in the outworking of our salvation, many things become clear that used to be confusing at best. For instance, Jesus describes a man who dies and comes before him, calling him "Lord" [Matthew 7:22-23]. This man clearly knew about Jesus and the power of his name. Now, let us be honest: which of us would *not* assume that a man who apparently *knows* Jesus, calls him "Lord" and demonstrates, through his *actions*, the power of God to heal those who suffer and free those who are oppressed by demons—which of us would not assume that this man has done his Father's will?

This man, who by Jesus' description could be mistaken for any of the "super Christians" of this or any time, comes before Jesus on the "last day." But what a strange response he receives from the One who "knows all men" [John 2:24]. "I never knew you!" This "knowing" seems to be the point. Jesus does not say: "You've done evil so you can't come in!." He *has* done evil, but what evil? Apparently his actions proceeded from some knowledge *about* Jesus and what he did, but those actions mask the deeper truth of his heart where the Father's will has not been done. His Father willed that the man come into eternal life by knowing and being known. The door to eternal life is closed to him. He cannot come in: *he is not known.*

When we understand that eternal life is knowing God and that we cannot know without a willingness to also be known, then it comes as no surprise to us that the word of eternal *death* is, "I never knew you"! But we need to be clear: those words did not put the man in Jesus' parable to death, nor did they snatch life from the young women who arrive late at the door of the bridegroom [Matthew 25:12]. The words "I don't know you" are simply a pronouncement of the truth of our condition apart from the regeneration of our very nature which occurs in the intimacy of a relationship with the living God characterized by knowing and being known.

The wonder of God's love for us is meant to melt our hard hearts and woo us into a loving response. This response is indispensable! What an amazing and literally awesome thing it is to realize that God cannot know me unless I respond—unless I bring myself to him, opening myself, expressing the truth of what I feel and think—yielding my mind and heart and will, my yesterday, my today, my tomorrow, to the One who is making all things new. Our Father takes it all into his heart.

It is not new information *about* me that he receives. He receives *me*!

When I enter the place where I desire to be known, my cry echoes the cry of the psalmist: "Search me, O God, and know my heart; test me and know my anxious thoughts" [Psalm 139:23]. As he comes to my cry and enters in, the life-creating action of his eternal love is made complete in me. His love has come in answer to my deepest heart's desire and met me in the whole truth of who I am. In this place of love's meeting there is nothing held back. Nothing screened out. No hiding place. All is out in the light of his love. My knowing is fulfilled. I know him. I know who I am. And I know that I am known. I experience the truth that I was made to know and be known by God. As the circuit of his love is completed in me, the sweetest truth of all rises up in my heart like the Morning Star:

It is only when I know that I am known, that I know I am loved. I taste the sweetness of this eternal truth now but will know the full flavour of it "then," when "face to face . . . I shall know fully, even as I am fully known" [1 Corinthians 13:12]!

Third Reflection In A Nutshell
"Choosing to Know and be Known"

For Jesus, intimacy with God the Father meant knowing and being known. This same knowing and being known is the ground of our intimacy with God. Just as God opens himself to be known, so must we if we are to be known by God intimately—in a personal relationship. Until we know that we are fully known we cannot know that we are fully loved.

Questions for reflection or discussion

1. "In Jesus we see that it is God's desire to be known." Are you aware of a desire to be known? What does being "known" mean to you? What barriers stand between you and your being known by other people and/or God?

2. We have seen that it is possible to know about God without really knowing him. But is it possible to "*know* God" without "knowing *about* him"? Reflect on what you have learned concerning the difference between "knowing about God" and "knowing God" especially as it concerns our call into a personal relationship with him.

3. From the viewpoint of our sinfulness, why would "knowing about God" be safer than "knowing God"?

4. ". . . obedience . . . lies at the heart of intimacy with God." Obviously, obedience is not always synonymous with love or with intimacy in the human to human sphere. What exactly is it about God that makes that intimacy with him impossible without our obedience? Why is it, do you think, that our obedience to God is a measure of our love of God?

5. We have come to this understanding concerning our relationship with God: "It is only when I know that I am known, that I know I am loved." In the light of this truth, reflect on how you might come to have a deeper awareness of God's love for you. Might this principle also apply in your human relationships?

PRAYING THE SCRIPTURE, PART 4
"On that day you will realize that I am in my Father, and you are in me, and I am in you."

This must be "that day", precious Lord: I know that you are in the Father. There is no pride in this place of knowing. The beautiful weight of this knowledge on my heart is almost too much to bear.

And as I enter into the love you share with your Father, I know that I am in you. The truth of your intimacy presses upon me and I can hardly draw a breath. Breathe for me, Holy Spirit, here in this place with you.

Yes, I know it is "that day". I know that you are in me. There is no such sweetness in the world. None in me. This sweetness in only found in you . . . in me.

This is the day that you have made, this day of knowing. "This day" is your day, Jesus. And so it is your day, Father. And yours, Holy Spirit. This is the day your love has made.

I do not ask for your love on this day. Just love your Father, Jesus, as you always do. Father, just love your Son. Search out their loving hearts, Holy Spirit. Know and be known. Give and receive. I won't say a word. I'll just be. In you. Please just be. In me. Don't love me. Just be. That is enough. I cannot bear to receive anything beyond the love you share this day.

There are no more words. There is just this day.

E pilogue

"Who may dwell upon your holy hill?"

A MEDITATION ON PSALM 15 & JOHN 8:3-11

I am suddenly a part of a familiar scene. I am in a crowd, listening, as a man of authority voices a question (it is our question), then his answer (it is our answer).

"Lord, who may dwell in your sanctuary? Who may abide upon your holy hill?" We gather in a circle around the man; everyone has the same eager question: "Do I qualify? Can I be there in that holy place?" At last he speaks. Here is the answer. This is the standard for all who would come in and find sanctuary: "whoever leads a blameless life".

Elaboration follows but I am deaf to it. "Whoever leads a blameless life": the weight of these words alone crushes me. And not just me, it seems. Every face falls. Anxious hands lifted in hope fall lifeless. Shoulders sag. All turn away to leave the scene, slowly, shaken.

As I go, I turn and see that at the center, where we were, there is another man, another questioner, and he is not alone. A woman kneels at his feet. (I remember now: we brought her here.) Her head is bowed and she is listening. She speaks, but only he can hear. Then his lips move, and though I do not hear him, I see his face as it lights on her. His light shines into my dark heart.

I turn in hope and see others turning. Together we come into a circle, but closer—much closer than before.

The woman is no longer bowed down; her face is lifted to him—to Jesus. "Neither do I condemn you," he says. He leans in toward the woman and says something more I cannot hear.

But I must hear. I need to know. I feel a great hunger. Slowly he turns to me: "Neither do I condemn you" he says, "go and sin no more"! To each in turn, all around the circle of those gathered, he repeats the words, "neither do I condemn you . . . go and sin no more".

As we go, he remains there with her. As we go, he goes with us. As we go, he has gone on ahead and is waiting.

A sweet song is throbbing in me: "Neither do I condemn you; neither do I condemn you; go and sin no more."

"Lord, who may dwell in your sanctuary?" I know something that I do not understand. I have received a penetrating word of love: "Neither do I condemn you." I have received a righteous word of truth: "Go and sin no more." I suddenly and simply know that if spoken in isolation neither word is Life. They must come together as a living, thirst-quenching song that Jesus sings in me. In him they are a single perfect Word, making me whole, setting me free. In him they are my answer—something I know but cannot understand.

"Lord, who may dwell in your sanctuary? Who may abide upon your Holy Hill?" The answer is spoken there in my heart where only He can hear. "You, Jesus. Only you."

"And you in me."

"And I in you."